Encyclopedia of
POLITICAL BUTTONS
United States 1896—1972

Including Prices, Campaign History, Technical Facts and Statistics

Ted Hake

Photography by Len Shackleford
Designed by Donald Afsanick
Edited by Gail D. Koller

HAKE'S AMERICANA & COLLECTIBLES
P.O. BOX 1444   YORK, PA 17405

Library of Congress Catalog Card Number 73-93793

ISBN 0-918708-06-0

PUBLISHER'S NOTE

This book is a black and white reprint of the full color edition published in 1974 and now out of print. The values shown in this book are from 1974 as the small number of books being printed did not make extensive typography changes possible. However, there have been significant price changes since 1974 as well as the publication of *Political Buttons Book II: 1920 - 1976* and *Political Buttons Book III: 1789 - 1916.* Together, the three volumes picture and catalogue over 12,000 presidential campaign items. In 1998, an experienced group of collectors and dealers completed price revisions for all 12,000 items. This 96 page "Revised Prices" supplement is available for $23.00 postpaid from the publisher.

TABLE OF CONTENTS

FOREWORD

Presidential campaign buttons offer a chance to collect colorful and historically significant mememtoes of America's past. This fact has not been lost on collectors and the hobby has experienced tremendous growth in the last ten years. Several national organizations exist to futher communication among collectors, hold collectors' meetings, initiate research projects, and report on reproductions of old buttons that can mislead collectors. These organizations are named the American Political Items Collectors (A.P.I.C.) and the Association for the Preservation of Political Americana (A.P.P.A.). Both groups issue informative newsletters for their members. Membership applications for both groups may be obtained by writing the author at P.O. Box 1444, York, PA 17405.

Celluloid buttons are the most popular presidential campaign items, but a beginning collector should not overlook the fact that campaign items have been used since the early 1800's and greatly proliferated after 1836. These items take the form of metal tokens, silk ribbons, clothing buttons, paper ballots, cloth flags and a wide assortment of other items such as plates, glasses, walking canes, paper lanterns, snuff boxes, etc. After 1856, ferrotype and cardboard photos were used in conjunction with brass tokens or pins to display the candidate's likeness. The prices for items from the 1800's cover as wide a range as do buttons, but it is possible to build a representative collection without investing great sums of money. Many of the common presidential tokens from 1840 to 1888 sell for ten dollars or even less. Considering the scarcity of many of the early items, they have been relatively undervalued compared to the celluloid buttons which attract most collectors because of their color and graphic qualities. The variety of presidential buttons seems unlimited. Even collectors with over five hundred different McKinley buttons continue to make new additions to their collections. This makes buttons a great hobby for collectors who enjoy the thrill of not knowing what may turn up next. Less than ten specimens of many of the rare buttons are known and yet each must have been manufactured in quantities of a thousand or more since they were intended for use by the public. No thought was given to the potential future value of political buttons as is the case with today's "limited edition" collectibles. Many of the buttons were thrown out, but many were put into the collections people began in 1896 when buttons were introduced as a great novelty. Slowly, but surely, as people with button accumulations, but no collecting interests, become aware of the potential value, the buttons are turned into cash and help meet the growing demands of collectors.

The prices of many scarce early presidential buttons have doubled and tripled in the past ten years while the values of common picture and name pins have increased slightly. This book is the first full color price guide and gives retail values for over four thousand buttons ranging from the most common to the most rare. Information is also provided to help dealers and collectors avoid the costly mistake of buying a button that has been reproduced. It is my hope that this book will open the hobby to new collectors and be a useful reseach tool and price guide for everyone interested in preserving the artifacts of America's presidential campaigns.

Introduction

BUTTON HISTORY

Celluloid pin back buttons were first made in 1896, but their manufacture rested on the invention of celluloid some twenty years earlier. According to J. Doyle DeWitt (A Century of Campaign Buttons 1789-1889), during the 1876 election campaign attempts were made to use newly discovered celluloid to produce campaign medalets. The image was to be imbedded in the celluloid by striking it with a die. At this time, the celluloid was too brittle and the efforts were abandoned.

Twelve years later, in the 1888 election, celluloid appeared for the first time as part of a device to be worn in support of a cause. The sole manufacturer appears to have been Baldwin & Gleason Co. Ltd., 61 B'way, N.Y. The firm specialized in advertising novelties and issued four different lapel studs picturing Harrison, Cleveland, Thurman, and Fisk. The pictures were made by printing ink directly on a celluloid disc. Celluloid was also being used for bookmarks and advertising cards by 1888.

Buttons, as made today, were first patented by the Whitehead & Hoag Co. of Newark, N.J. Celluloid was used as a thin, transparent covering to protect the paper the image was printed on. Three patent dates appeared on early W&H buttons. The December 3, 1893 patent was filed by Amanda M. Lougee of Boston, Massachusetts. W&H apparently purchased rights to this patent within the next two years to protect their other claims. The patent was actually for a cloth and metal clothing button and the design used in assembling the button so that the exposed face was "composed wholly of cloth and without visible metal...."

The next patent field December 6, 1895, established the design of the reverse side of celluloid buttons. Issued as a "jewelry" patent to George B. Adams, assignor to W&H, the patent specified a shell with a marginal rim which formed a chamber and contained a continuous piece of wire with both a holding portion and a free end lying in the same plane.

The final patent was filed March 23, 1896, and issued July 21, 1896, again to George B. Adams. Six claims were made, each varying slightly from Claim I which reads:

> In a badge pin or button, in combination, with a shell having a marginal rim or bead, a covering bearing an inscription, design, emblem, or the like, over said shell and having its edges turned down over said marginal rim, a ring or collet in said shell placed over the edge of said covering to hold or secure the latter in position, and a bar or pin having one of its ends bent to form a holding portion adapted to be secured in said ring or collet, substantially as and for the purposes set forth.

Regardless of the day in 1896 actual manufacture of buttons began, W&H produced an amazing variety and number that first year. Production was stimulated by the intensity of the McKinley and Bryan presidential campaign battle over the issue of the gold and silver coinage ratio. Also, the manufacturers of candy, chewing gum, and tobacco were soon offering free buttons with their products.

Buttons were a natural extension of the insert cards which had been in use for years and pictured athletes, Indians, statesmen or any other popular subject. Button collectors of the day soon had an equally wide variety of subjects to collect. The American Pepsin Gum Co. and Sweet Caporal Cigarettes offered the widest variety of button sets.

Along with W&H, other companies were soon producing well designed and colorful buttons. The major producers included American Art Works, Coshocton, Ohio; Bastian Bros. (who eventually purchased W&H), Rochester, N.Y.; St. Louis Button Co., St. Louis, Mo.; and Torsh and Franz, Baltimore, Md. Hundreds of button jobbers were also placing their names on buttons, although the buttons were actually produced by the manufacturing companies.

From 1896 to 1920, button designing was at its peak. The designs and wide variety of color inks resulted in exceptional beauty rarely achieved in later years. The demise of quality celluloid buttons parallels the development of a process that resulted in lithographed tin buttons. Printing color on tin was technically feasible in the 1880's when the process was used to produce several thousand varieties of plug tobacco tags. These small flat pieces of tin showed the name of the product and were fastened to it by two small pointed prongs. An occasional presidential campaign item was also produced in this manner, but with only one prong which had a small hole in it for a straight pin which held the item to clothing. This was a cumbersome method of attachment, but by the 1920 presidential campaign the problem was solved with the introduction of mass produced lithographed tin buttons.

BUTTON HISTORY

Lithographed buttons are stamped and shaped by a die from one large sheet of tin upon which many images of the button are printed. The process is quicker and less expensive than the process required to produce celluloid (now acetate) covered buttons. Currently, celluloid buttons seem saved from extinction only because economics require lithographed buttons be produced in a minimum lot of 10,000 to be profitable to the manufacturer.

From 1920, lithographed buttons were produced in ever greater quantites. The Green Duck Co. of Chicago consistently has been the largest manufacturer. To the collector who concentrates on color and design, lithographed buttons are a poor second to celluloid. Usually only two or three colors are used and design is held to a minimum. Lithographed buttons are also very easily scratched or may suffer paint chips if not handled properly.

During the 1930's and 1940's two trends began that persist today and trouble collector's artistic sensibilities. First, more and more buttons were made two or three inches in diameter. This seems to be the influence of modern advertising techniques. The goal apparently is easy readability, but any favorable results in this direction must surely be voided by people's natural reluctance to be seen with a three inch button hanging from their coat. These buttons get little use in public and are scorned by collectors who object to the space they require and poor design.

The second trend is the nearly exclusive use of red, white, and blue colors for political buttons. The result is that buttons for all the candidates look identical and collectors have little opportunity to acquire attractive items.

Fortunately, the button revival of the 1960's, combined with the advent of pop and psychedelic art, has started to reverse these trends. Buttons produced for ecology issues and in opposition to the Viet Nam war feature more complex designs and use color more freely. Unfortunately current presidential campaign buttons are largely limited to faces and names rather than symbolic representation of issues which the turn of the century designers achieved so skillfully. The 1972 buttons of George McGovern do show more color and design variety. Hopefully this trend will continue in future presidential elections.

Introduction

NUMBERING SYSTEM

Each major party candidate has been assigned a code made up of the first three letters of his last name, and each item has been numbered. Thus, any particular button can be referred to by listing the three code letters and the item number. For example, WIL-16 refers to item number 16 in the Woodrow Wilson section. The only exception to this system is that the code letters for Franklin Roosevelt are FDR. These codes appear at the top of the first page of each candidate's section.

The codes for the minor party buttons are derived either from the candidate's name or some combination of letters from the party name. Thus, PRO-3 refers to item number 3 in the Prohibition Party section.

ABBREVIATIONS

Between the item number and the price of the item there may be one or more letters that give additional information about the item. If the item is something other than a celluloid button, these letters tell how the item was used, what it is made of, and whether or not the item has been reproduced. See the section on REPRODUCTIONS for an explanation of how the information in this book can help determine whether a button is original or a reproduced version.

A-Attachment (usual for a car)
B-Brass
C-Cardboard
D-One button from a set
E-Enamel
F-Rubber
H-Clothing button
I-Mirror
K-Silk
L-Lithographed tin button
M-Mechanical
N-See Notes
O-O'Hara Watch Dial Co., porcelain stud
P-Plastic
R-Paper
S-Lapel stud
T-Tin
U-Celluloid
W-Wood
Y-Lithographed tin reproduction has been made
Z-Celluloid reproduction has been made

PHOTO SIZES AND ARRANGEMENT

All buttons are pictured extremely close to actual size. The items for each candidate are generally arranged in the following order: jugates of all sizes, large single picture buttons, 1¼" single picture buttons, ⅞" and smaller single picture buttons, buttons showing presidential candidate with state candidates, large name buttons, 1¼" presidential and vice-presidential name buttons, 1¼" slogan buttons, ⅞" presidential and vice-presidential name buttons, ⅞" presidential name buttons, ⅞" slogan buttons, novelty items, memorial items, and addenda, if any.

GLOSSARY

Brummagen—a showy, but worthless and inferior thing. This is the American Political Items Collectors Organization's term for a reproduced political button.

Celluloid Button—made of a paper with a celluloid covering. Both are wrapped around a metal disc and held in place by a metal rim on the back of the item. As celluloid is flammable, acetate is now the common covering that protects the paper.

Collet—the metal rim on the back or a celluloid button or mirror.

Ferrotypes—one of the photographic processes of the 1860's in which the photographic emulsion was spread on a thin piece of iron. Presidential items were usually made by placing a small ferrotype in a quarter size brass disc that could be tied to the coat lapel by a ribbon.

Foxing-brown—stain marks under the celluloid covering of a button usually caused by water or excessive moisture rusting the metal disc under the button paper.

Jugate—side by side pictures of the presidential and vice-presidential candidates on the same item.

Lapel stud—usually round in shape like a button, but with a metal shank on the back to hold the item in a button hole.

Litho.—a button stamped from a sheet of lithographed tin. There is no collet on the back and the pin is held in only by the curvature of the metal rim. Commonly in use after 1916, but lithographed buttons for candidates from 1896 to 1916 are almost always modern reproductions of items that were originally made of celluloid.

Mechanical—an item usually made of brass that moves by means of a spring. The term is loosely applied to any item that has moving parts.

CONDITION AND GRADING

Celluloid buttons are nearly immune to dirt and age, but quite vulnerable to moisture. The term "foxing" applies to the brown spots or stains which occur if water or moisture rusts the metal disc under the button paper. A few light spots decrease the value about 25%, but if the stains are large or dark, the value rapidly decreases to almost nothing. Rusting on a lithographed tin button has the same effect on value.

Other common forms of damage include scratches, dents, cracks in the celluloid, and peeling wherein the celluloid begins to separate from the paper, usually along the rim. This sort of damage decreases the value by 50% or more depending upon the extent of damage. Many collectors will not buy damaged buttons even if the price is a small fraction of that for the same button in perfect condition.

PRICES

The prices listed in this book are retail prices for buttons with no damage whatsoever. Factors considered in arriving at a a price for each button are: whether it is a jugate, picture, slogan or name button; age, rarity, and demand. Beauty, age, and the degree of novelty are all factors that affect the pricing of novelty and mechanical items.

While this book contains prices for over four thousand items, it is by no means complete and no book on the subject ever will be since new finds are a common occurence in the hobby. However, prices for buttons not shown in this book can be deduced by comparison with other similar buttons for any given candidate. There is not a wide range of price fluctuation for buttons that simply show a candidate's picture or name and nothing more. Such a comparison would be inappropriate only if the button not pictured in this book would have a catchy slogan, exceptionally colorful artwork, or some unusual pictorial representation of a political issue.

When selling presidential buttons to a dealer, the seller can reasonably expect 40% to 50% of the prices listed here for the more common items that are in less demand and 60% for the rarer items that are in more demand. Factors that the dealer must consider when buying presidential buttons include: the demand for the buttons being offered, the condition of the buttons, whether he already has the same buttons in his stock, the percentage of saleable vs. non-saleable buttons in the lot, whether there are some rare items he can sell quickly to get his investment back, and the length of time it will take to sell the entire lot. These factors, plus the fact that the dealer's expenses and profit come from his mark-up, account for the discrepancy between his buying prices and the retail prices in this book.

The demand for presidential buttons has steadily increased and is reflected most in the rising prices for the unusual and rare buttons. The common picture and name pins have also shown steady increases, but at a slower rate and they are still very much in reach of the collector with a limited collecting budget. Presidential button collecting is a hobby pursued by most people for enjoyment, but it is comforting to know that buttons bought in the past have increased in value and provided an enjoyable hedge against inflation. With the growth of collectors' organizations, increased leisure time, and the increased emphasis on our past as America's Bi-Centennial approaches, there is every reason to expect continued increases in the value of presidential buttons.

REPRODUCTIONS

The need to beware of reproduced political buttons is the only unpleasant aspect of button collecting. Unfortunately, whenever any item becomes valuable someone is around to make a cheap imitation. The intent of the people who reproduce presidential campaign items is to defraud collectors, for it is a simple matter to mark the new buttons with the word "reproduction" or the current year.

The Hobby Protection Act, signed into law November 29, 1973, is designed to protect collectors from the manufacture of a variety of imitation hobby items. From that date on, the manufacture in the United States, or the importation into the United States, for introduction into or distribution in commerce of any imitation political item which is not plainly and permanently marked with the calendar year in which such item was manufactured, is unlawful and is an unfair or deceptive act or practice under the Federal Trade Commission Act. Some major provisions of the law now make it unlawful to sell a "hobby item which is a reproduction of a political button, poster, sticker, literature, or any advertisement used in any political cause, and which is not plainly marked with the calendar year in which such a reproduction was manufactured..." The term reproduction is defined as "imitation or copy", and the Federal Trade Commission is authorized to prevent any person from violating the provisions of the Act. This law should end the flood of political buttons intended to fool the collector, and this book can aid collectors in identifying reproductions already on the market.

All the original lithographed tin buttons in this book are identified by the letter "L" following the item number. All buttons not designated by the letter "L" are original buttons made of celluloid. Additional letter abbreviations following the item number tell if that particular button has been issued as a reproduction. A letter "Y" means a lithographed tin reproduction has been made and a "Z" means a celluloid reproduction has been made. In a few cases, "YZ" is used to indicate both a lithographed tin and a celluloid reproduction has been made.

All available information has been used to identify the buttons in this book which have been issued as reproductions. The problem of identifying reproductions is complicated by the fact that a substantial number of buttons after 1916 were originally issued in both lithographed tin and celluloid varieties. Thus, if a celluloid button is shown in the book and a lithographed variety is found, the lithographed variety is not necessarily a reproduction. Only if the letter "Y" is shown as part of the code for that particular button should it be assumed that the lithographed button is a reproduction. In the case of original celluloid buttons which have been reproduced in celluloid, there are so many different individual characteristics about the reproductions that a separate book would be required to explain them. One common fallacy is that original buttons are marked by an imprint of the union shop insignia on the back of the button and that reproduced buttons do not carry this "union bug." The presence or absence of this union insignia depends simply on whether or not the person or organization that orders the button wants to spend extra money to have the union imprint which means that the button was made in a union shop.

As a general rule, if a "Y" or "Z" appears after a button in this book, be extremely careful when purchasing a button that looks the same. If expert advice is not available, be sure that the button is purchased only with the understanding that a full refund will be made if it is later determined that the button is a reproduction. It may be necessary to require a written guarantee and have the seller put some mark on the back of the button so there can be no question later on that a button a refund is requested for is the same one originally owned by the seller. Be especially cautious of the dealer who sells commonly recognized reproductions of other types of collectibles and yet makes assurances that his presidential buttons are not reproductions. Reputable dealers will not handle any type of reproduction for they know that somewhere down the line the item will be represented as genuine and used to defraud a collector with more enthusiasm than experience. More information about reproductions can be obtained by joining the presidential button collectors' organizations mentioned in the Foreword.

NOTES

McKINLEY
204. Brass horse blanket pin about six inches long.
224. Missing paper photos on the wings. If photos are on the item the value is $100.
267. Brass holder for wood matches with striker on the bottom lid.
302. Push lever at top and either McKinley or Bryan appears in the doorway.
304. Button slides down to reveal "McKinley" in brass letters.

BRYAN
13. Item can be turned so either Bryan and Sewell or McKinley and Hobart appear.
25. Also shows McKinley and Roosevelt when rotated.
363. Push lever at top and either Bryan or McKinley appears in the doorway.

THEODORE ROOSEVELT
59. Roosevelt and Johnson jugates from 1912 are extremely rare.
187. Theodore Roosevelt and Robert LaFollette of Wisconsin.
246. 248. 250. These three were issued by cigarette companies.

TAFT
14. A "salesmen's safety pin" which shows both candidates and indicates the wearer is a neutral.
34. The original 1912 version of this pin has been reproduced also.
146. Also issued with the names of other states.
199. Aluminum bookmark.

COX
1. The Cox-Roosevelt jugate is the most highly valued, but not the rarest presidential button. Of the four design varieties known, Whitehead & Hoad made two and the St. Louis Button Co. and the Reading Badge Co. each made one. The size varieties are ⅝", ⅞" and 1¼". Less than fifty specimens of this button are known to be in existence.

COOLIDGE
90. This is a "clicker" or noise maker.

HOOVER
74. This is a "clicker" or noise maker.

FRANKLIN ROOSEVELT
212. Also issued with the names of other states.
213. Also issued with the names of other states.

LANDON
61. This is an anti-Landon item.

NOTES

WILLKIE

10. A "salesmen's safety pin" which shows both candidates and indicates the wearer is neutral.

27. The reproduction of this button does not have eagles on the sides.

174. It is uncertain for whom this pin was issued.

DEWEY

129. It is uncertain for whom this pin was issued.

EISENHOWER

48. Issued in other languages.

49. Issued in other languages.

107. Issued as a set of the forty-eight states.

200. 203. Cloth items made in India.

KENNEDY

131.-134. These items were issued after the 1960 election.

NIXON

19. Issued in other languages.

101. Issued in other languages.

GOLDWATER

3. Issued in other languages.

SOCIALIST

25. This is not a campaign item.

WILLIAM McKINLEY — REPUBLICAN

Campaigns	1896	1900
	WON	WON
Electoral Votes	271	292
Popular Votes	7,113,734	7,219,828
Running Mates	GARRET A. HOBART	THEODORE ROOSEVELT
Conventions	ST. LOUIS	PHILADELPHIA
Birth	NILES, OHIO, JAN. 29, 1843	
Death	SEPT. 14, 1901	

Campaign buttons made their debut in the 1896 election and Republican candidates William McKinley and Garret Hobart were championed by over eight hundred known varieties of buttons and small novelty items. The immense quantities and varieties of McKinley buttons have created the cituation in which many of the oldest presidential buttons are less valuable than buttons from some more recent campaigns. Most single picture or slogan buttons range from four to ten dollars and most jugates from five to twenty dollars. However, many clever and well-designed buttons were also produced and these are highly valued by collectors.

Common slogans on the buttons include "protection to American industry" and "sound money". Protection referred to the Republican's desire for a high tariff favored by the Eastern industrialized section of the country. "Sound money" meant the country's monetary system should be based solely on gold rather than a duel system of silver and gold in a ratio of sixteen to one. The Republicans became known as "Goldbugs" and the Democrats as "Silverbugs". The "Goldbug" became one of the most frequently used symbols. It was pictured on many buttons and also issued as three dimensional items ranging from half inch lapel studs up to six inch horse blanket pins. Satirical anti-Bryan items were also issued. Many of these used the slogan "NIT" which meant "Not In Trust" and indicated the Republican opposition to the sixteen to one coinage ratio. Other slogans such as "prosperity" and "a full dinner pail" promised relief from the economic hard times the country experienced during the presidency of Grover Cleveland, McKinley's Democratic predecessor from 1888 to 1892.

McKinley's campaign manager, Mark Hanna, ran one of the best organized campaigns up to that time. He had McKinley stay at home in Canton, Ohio to conduct "the front porch campaign" while William Jennings Bryan raced around the country. Hanna raised millions of dollars and gave much of it to state delegations for train fare to Canton. The railroads also offered reduced rates so ordinary citizens could visit the candidate. Thousands of people made the pilgrimage, and on one particular day McKinley addressed an audience of thirty thousand. McKinley won the election aided by some businessmen who advised their employees not to come to work if Bryan was elected.

McKinley's Vice-President, Garret Hobart, was greatly admired for his intelligence and hard work, but he died in office in November, 1899. Theodore Roosevelt was chosen by party leaders as the 1900 Vice-Presidential candidate. An improving economy and the pledge of "four more years of the full dinner pail," won a second term for McKinley.

In September, 1901, McKinley spoke at the Pan-American Exposition in Buffalo, N.Y. A public reception was held at the Temple of Music and Leon Czolgosz, an anarchist who carried a gun concealed in his bandaged hand, stepped before McKinley and shot him twice. After eight days, McKinley succumbed to gangrene on September 14, and Theodore Roosevelt became President.

1—A—$20.00

2—$6.00   3—$12.00   4—$8.00   5—Y—$20.00

6—$10.00   7—$5.00   8—$175.00   9—$15.00

10—S—$8.00   11—S—$8.00   12—S—$8.00   13—S—$8.00   14—S—$6.00   15—S—$15.00

16—$5.00   17—$5.00   18—$12.00   19—S—$10.00   20—S—$5.00   21—S—$5.00

22—$20.00

23—$35.00

24—$6.00

25—$6.00

26—Y—$6.00

27—$6.00

28—$6.00

29—Y—$6.00

30—$6.00

31—$6.00

32—$15.00

33—$12.00

34—$6.00

35—$8.00

36—$12.00

37—$8.00

38—$35.00

39—Z—$15.00

40—Z—$15.00

41—$65.00

WILLIAM McKINLEY 1896, 1900 CODE: MAC

42—$15.00   43—$6.00   44-L—$8.00   45—$6.00

46—$5.00   47—$6.00

48—$8.00   50—$5.00

51—$6.00   52—$6.00

49—$15.00

53—$5.00   54—$5.00

55—$5.00   57—$5.00

56—C—$25.00

16

58—$8.00

59—$6.00

60—$8.00

61—$5.00

62—$10.00

63—$10.00

64—$15.00

65—$30.00

66—$10.00

67—$6.00

68—$75.00

69—Y—$18.00

70—$6.00

71—$6.00

72—$5.00

73—$5.00

74—$5.00

75—$5.00

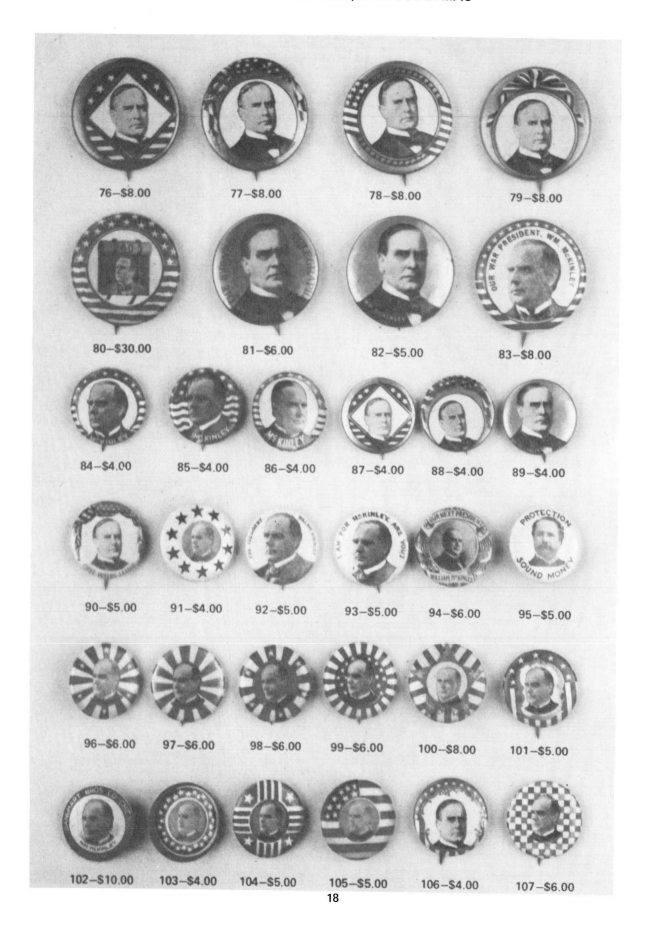

76—$8.00   77—$8.00   78—$8.00   79—$8.00

80—$30.00   81—$6.00   82—$5.00   83—$8.00

84—$4.00   85—$4.00   86—$4.00   87—$4.00   88—$4.00   89—$4.00

90—$5.00   91—$4.00   92—$5.00   93—$5.00   94—$6.00   95—$5.00

96—$6.00   97—$6.00   98—$6.00   99—$6.00   100—$8.00   101—$5.00

102—$10.00   103—$4.00   104—$5.00   105—$5.00   106—$4.00   107—$6.00

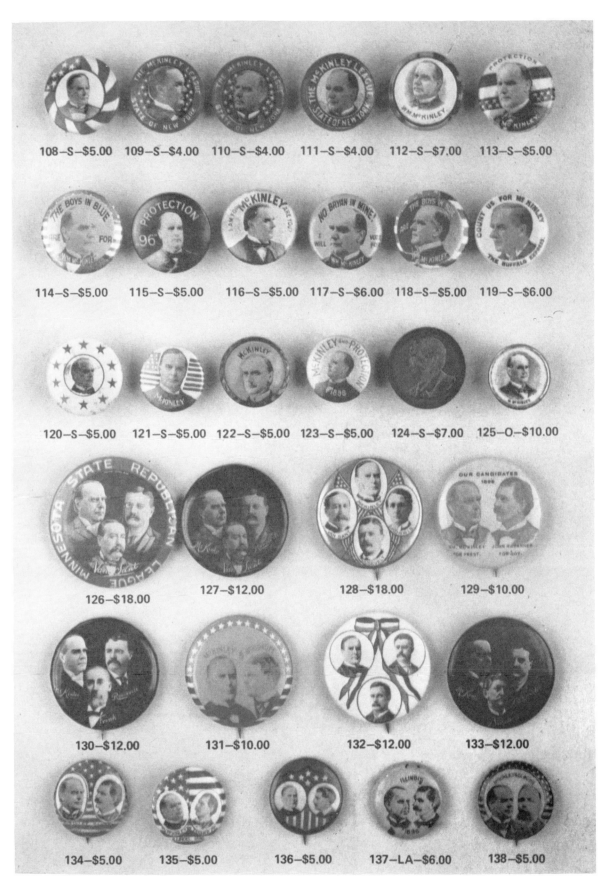

108—S—$5.00   109—S—$4.00   110—S—$4.00   111—S—$4.00   112—S—$7.00   113—S—$5.00

114—S—$5.00   115—S—$5.00   116—S—$5.00   117—S—$6.00   118—S—$5.00   119—S—$6.00

120—S—$5.00   121—S—$5.00   122—S—$5.00   123—S—$5.00   124—S—$7.00   125—O—$10.00

126—$18.00   127—$12.00   128—$18.00   129—$10.00

130—$12.00   131—$10.00   132—$12.00   133—$12.00

134—$5.00   135—$5.00   136—$5.00   137—LA—$6.00   138—$5.00

139—$100.00

140—$75.00

141—$25.00

142—$4.00

143—$10.00

144—$14.00

145—$15.00

146—$6.00

147—$5.00

148—$4.00

149—$12.00

150—$12.00

151—$8.00

152—$5.00

153—$5.00

154—$6.00

155—$5.00

156—$5.00

157—$4.00

158—$6.00

159—$4.00

160—$4.00

161—$3.00

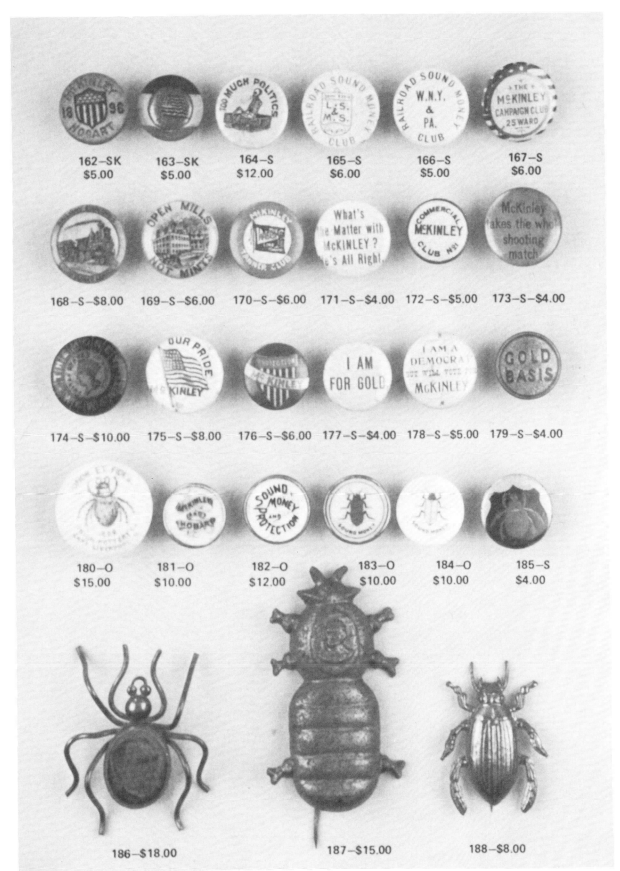

162—SK
$5.00

163—SK
$5.00

164—S
$12.00

165—S
$6.00

166—S
$5.00

167—S
$6.00

168—S—$8.00   169—S—$6.00   170—S—$6.00   171—S—$4.00   172—S—$5.00   173—S—$4.00

174—S—$10.00   175—S—$8.00   176—S—$6.00   177—S—$4.00   178—S—$5.00   179—S—$4.00

180—O
$15.00

181—O
$10.00

182—O
$12.00

183—O
$10.00

184—O
$10.00

185—S
$4.00

186—$18.00   187—$15.00   188—$8.00

189—M—$50.00 190—$45.00 191—$45.00 192—M $35.00

193—$45.00 194—S—$30.00 195—S—$25.00 196—S—$10.00 197—S—$10.00

198—$15.00 199—$10.00

200—$15.00 201—$8.00

204—N—$35.00

202—S—$17.00 203—$6.00 205—$6.00 206—S—$18.00

WILLIAM McKINLEY 1896, 1900 CODE: MAC

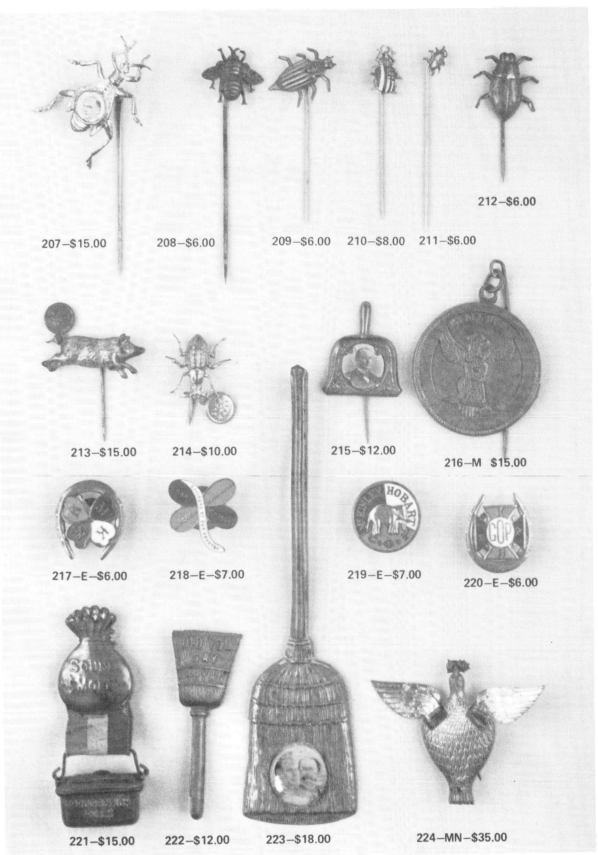

207—$15.00   208—$6.00   209—$6.00   210—$8.00   211—$6.00   212—$6.00

213—$15.00   214—$10.00   215—$12.00   216—M $15.00

217—E—$6.00   218—E—$7.00   219—E—$7.00   220—E—$6.00

221—$15.00   222—$12.00   223—$18.00   224—MN—$35.00

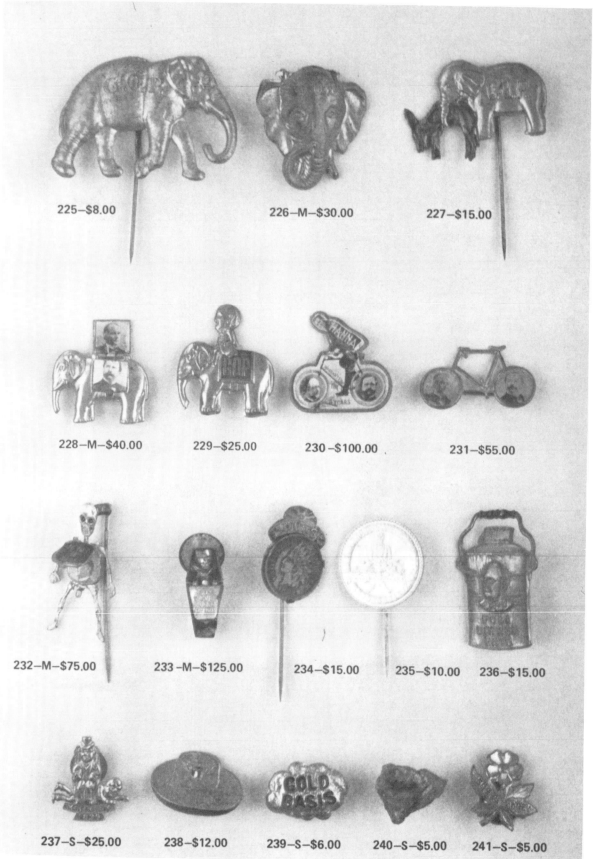

225—$8.00

226—M—$30.00

227—$15.00

228—M—$40.00

229—$25.00

230—$100.00

231—$55.00

232—M—$75.00

233—M—$125.00

234—$15.00

235—$10.00

236—$15.00

237—S—$25.00

238—$12.00

239—S—$6.00

240—S—$5.00

241—S—$5.00

242—$8.00   243—$6.00   244—$10.00   245—$5.00

246—$6.00   247—$6.00   248—S—$7.00   249—$8.00

250—$14.00   251—M—$20.00   252—$6.00   253—$4.00

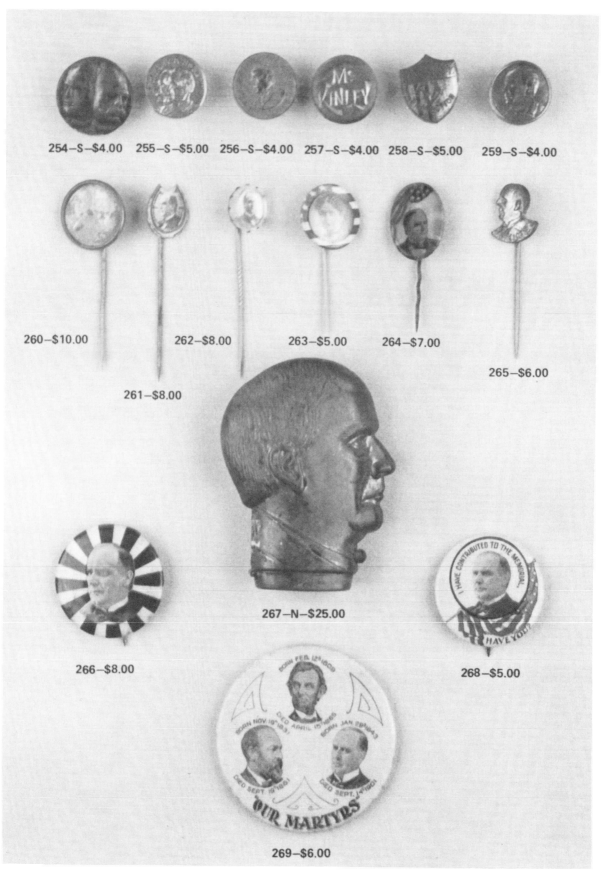

254—S—$4.00   255—S—$5.00   256—S—$4.00   257—S—$4.00   258—S—$5.00   259—S—$4.00

260—$10.00   262—$8.00   263—$5.00   264—$7.00

                                                                    265—$6.00

261—$8.00

267—N—$25.00

266—$8.00

268—$5.00

269—$6.00

270—$3.00   271—$4.00   272—$4.00

273—$3.00   275—$3.00

274—$3.00

276—$2.00   277—$3.00   278—$3.00

279—$3.00   280—$4.00

281—$25.00

282—$20.00

283—$75.00

284—$6.00

285—$12.00

286—$20.00

287—$65.00

288—$18.00

289—$22.00

290—$150.00

291—$12.00

292—$30.00

293—$15.00

294—S—$7.00

295—$75.00

296—$18.00

297—$18.00

298—$30.00

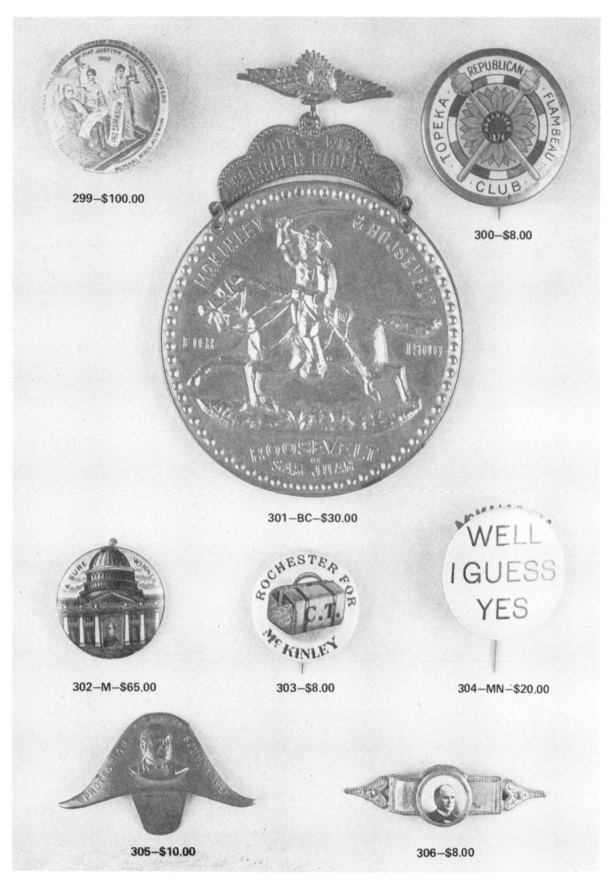

299—$100.00

300—$8.00

301—BC—$30.00

302—M—$65.00

303—$8.00

304—MN—$20.00

305—$10.00

306—$8.00

WILLIAM JENNINGS BRYAN — DEMOCRAT

Campaigns	1896	1900	1908
	LOST	LOST	LOST
Electoral Votes	176	155	162
Popular Votes	6,516,722	6,358,160	6,410,665
Running Mates	ARTHUR SEWELL	ADLAI E. STEVENSON	JOHN W. KERN
Conventions	CHICAGO	KANSAS CITY, MO.	DENVER
Birth	SALEM, ILL., MARCH 19, 1860		
Death	JULY 26, 1925		

William Jennings Bryan was elected to Congress in 1890 with an established reputation as the "silver-tongued orator from Nebraska". Six years later at the Democratic convention in Chicago, he delivered his vehement attack on the gold standard in his famous "cross of gold" speech. The next day the delegates rewarded him with the nomination for President. Bryan made an extensive tour of the country campaigning as the representative of the common man and advocating the coinage silver and gold in a ratio of sixteen to one. Bryan lost the election but was nominated for a second try in 1900.

Despite evidence the gold standard had improved the nation's economy, Bryan's view remained unchanged. He had a tendency to see all questions in terms of a struggle between good and evil and there was little flexibility in his philosophy. The only new issue in 1900 was the question of expansion and Bryan's anti-imperialism was in conflict with a nation eager to benefit from the spoils of the Spanish-American War. Bryan lost the 1900 election and went on to lose a third time in 1908.

Bryan continued as a party leader and supported Woodrow Wilson in 1912. He became Wilson's Secretary of State in 1913, but resigned in 1915 because his pacifist philosophy was in conflict with America's increasing involvement in World War I. In 1925, Bryan participated in the trial of John T. Scopes, a teacher indicted for teaching the theory of evolution in violation of Tennessee law. Bryan was a fundamentalist who had helped to draft similar legislation, but a severe cross-examination by lawyer Clarence Darrow exposed Bryan's narrow views and ended his career with a humiliating defeat shortly before he died.

The value of buttons of Bryan are comparable to McKinley buttons. Most single picture buttons range from five to fifteen dollars and jugates from seven to twenty dollars. Bryan and Kern 1¼" jugates are somewhat scarcer than other size jugates and are priced higher. Buttons done in a cartoon style or referring to the "cross of gold" speech also command a higher price. Several 1908 buttons were done in exceptionally nice colors and designs reflecting the art nouveau style of the era. A large number of mechanical and novelty items were issued to represent the contest between "Silverbugs" and "Goldbugs." Usually these items were given a silver finish to represent the Democrats and made in brass to represent the Republicans. The Republicans also circulated "Bryan money" which were large heavy discs of white metal designed as satirical representations of ten cent pieces or silver dollars. These carried slogans such as "United Snakes of America" and "16 to 1 NIT (Not In Trust)." The 1896 and 1900 elections produced more unusual and intriguiging items than any other election from 1896 to 1972.

1-S—$15.00

2—S—$14.00

3—S—$25.00

4—$24.00

5—S—$22.00

6—S—$16.00

7—S—$18.00

8—S—$15.00

9—S—$22.00

10—Y—$20.00

11—$20.00

12—$30.00

13—MN—$35.00

14—$12.00 15—$12.00 16—$14.00 17—$14.00 18—$14.00

19—$18.00

20—$18.00

WILLIAM JENNINGS BRYAN 1896, 1900, 1908 CODE: BRY

21—$40.00

22—$30.00

23—$15.00

24—$15.00

25—MN—$65.00

26—$15.00

27—$18.00

28—$15.00

29—$18.00

30—$20.00

31—$12.00

32—$12.00

33—$12.00

34—$12.00

35—$28.00   36—$28.00   37—$26.00   38—$75.00

39—$30.00   40—$28.00   41—$28.00   42—$30.00

43—$28.00   44—$22.00   45—$20.00   46—$20.00

47—$20.00   48—$24.00   49—$18.00   50—$18.00   51—$18.00

52—$40.00   53—L—$12.00   54—$12.00   55—$12.00

56—$18.00   57—$15.00   58—$18.00   59—$15.00

60—$12.00   61—$12.00   62—Y—$15.00   63—$18.00   64—$14.00

65—Z—$10.00   66—$10.00   67—$10.00   68—$10.00   69—$10.00   70—$12.00

71—$12.00   72—$10.00   73—$10.00   74—$10.00   75—$10.00   76—$14.00

77–$35.00

78–$25.00

79–$25.00

80–$30.00

81–$22.00

82–$24.00

83–Z–$24.00

84–$24.00

85–Z–$28.00

86–$26.00

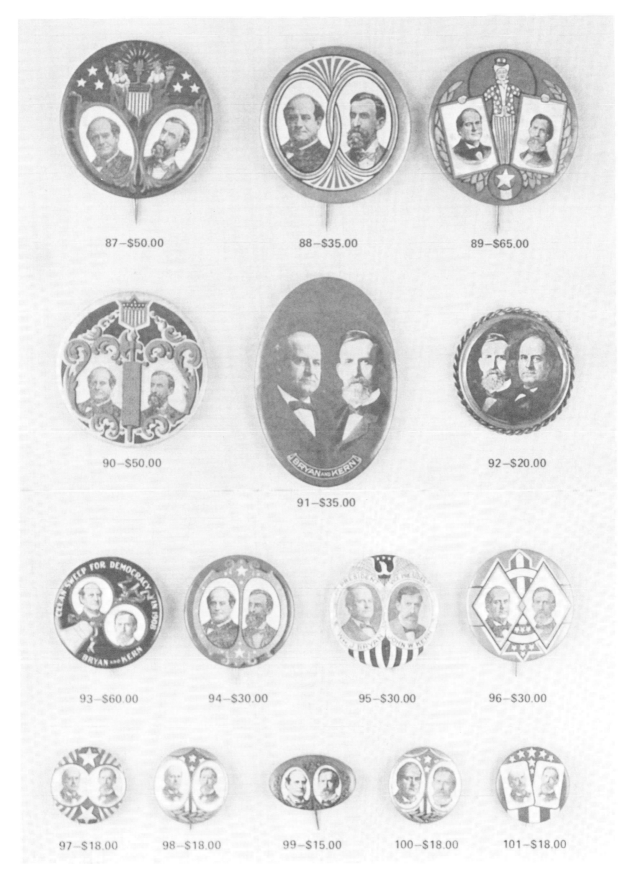

87—$50.00   88—$35.00   89—$65.00

90—$50.00   92—$20.00

91—$35.00

93—$60.00   94—$30.00   95—$30.00   96—$30.00

97—$18.00   98—$18.00   99—$15.00   100—$18.00   101—$18.00

102—$45.00

103—$28.00

104—$22.00

105—$28.00

106—$12.00

107—$14.00

108—$12.00

109—$12.00

110-Z—$10.00

111—$12.00

112—$75.00

113—$12.00

114—$12.00

115—$12.00

116—$10.00

117-Y—$20.00

WILLIAM JENNINGS BRYAN 1896, 1900, 1908 CODE: BRY

118—$45.00

119—$40.00

120—$40.00

121—$20.00

122—$20.00

123—$15.00

124—$65.00

125—$15.00

126—$10.00

127—$10.00

129—$25.00

128—$14.00

130—$14.00

131—$14.00

132—$7.00

133—$8.00

134—$10.00

WILLIAM JENNINGS BRYAN 1896, 1900, 1908 CODE: BRY

135—$6.00 136—$25.00 137—$8.00 138—$8.00

139—$6.00 140—$8.00 141—$5.00 142—$6.00

143—$5.00 144—$5.00 145—$6.00 146—$8.00

147—$6.00 148—$15.00 149—$5.00 150—$6.00

151—$1.00 152—$8.00 153—$6.00 154—$10.00

WILLIAM JENNINGS BRYAN 1896, 1900, 1908 CODE: BRY

155—$8.00   156—$12.00   157—$8.00   158—$12.00

159—$10.00   160—$10.00   161—$8.00   162-L-$8.00

163—$8.00   164—$10.00   165—$6.00   166—$6.00

167—Y—$6.00   168—$6.00   169—$10.00   170—$8.00

171—$35.00   172—$12.00   173—$10.00   174—$8.00

WILLIAM JENNINGS BRYAN 1896, 1900, 1908 CODE: BRY

175—O—$10.00   176—S—$15.00   177—S—$15.00   178—S—$12.00   179—S—$6.00

180—$5.00   181—$6.00   182—$6.00   183—$5.00   184—$10.00

185—$10.00   186—$6.00   187—$10.00   188—$6.00   189—$6.00   190—$8.00

191—$6.00   192—$8.00   193—$5.00   194—$5.00   195—$6.00   196—$5.00

197—$6.00   198—$5.00   199—$10.00   200—$6.00   201—$8.00   202—$6.00

203—$6.00   204—$6.00   205—$8.00   206—$8.00   207—$6.00   208—$8.00

209—$6.00   210—$6.00   211—$8.00   212—$6.00   213—$6.00   214—$8.00

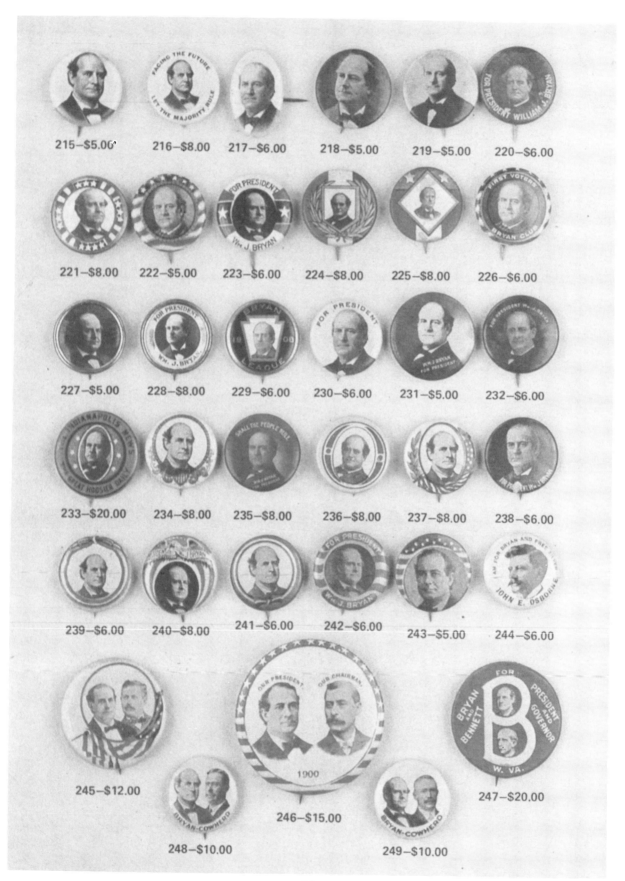

215—$5.00 216—$8.00 217—$6.00 218—$5.00 219—$5.00 220—$6.00

221—$8.00 222—$5.00 223—$6.00 224—$8.00 225—$8.00 226—$6.00

227—$5.00 228—$8.00 229—$6.00 230—$6.00 231—$5.00 232—$6.00

233—$20.00 234—$8.00 235—$8.00 236—$8.00 237—$8.00 238—$6.00

239—$6.00 240—$8.00 241—$6.00 242—$6.00 243—$5.00 244—$6.00

245—$12.00 248—$10.00 246—$15.00 249—$10.00 247—$20.00

250–S–$10.00   251–$5.00   252–$8.00   253–$12.00   254–$12.00   255–$8.00

256–$60.00   257–$8.00   258–$10.00

259–$5.00   260–$5.00   261–$5.00   262–$10.00

263–$25.00   264–$75.00   265–$100.00   266–$15.00

267–$10.00   268–$12.00   269–$10.00   270–$5.00   271–$5.00

272–$30.00   273–$5.00   274–$5.00   275–$10.00   276–$10.00

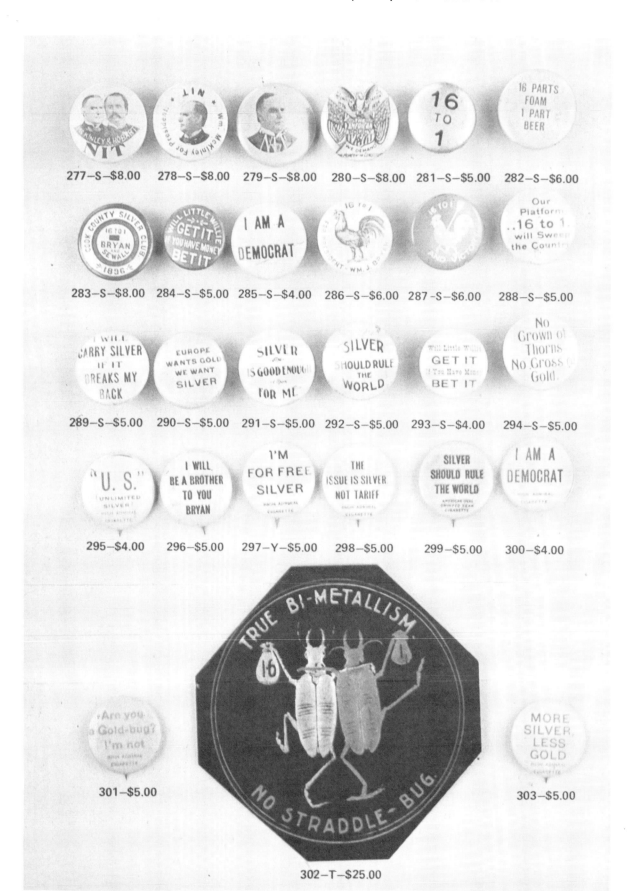

277-S-$8.00   278-S-$8.00   279-S-$8.00   280-S-$8.00   281-S-$5.00   282-S-$6.00

283-S-$8.00   284-S-$5.00   285-S-$4.00   286-S-$6.00   287-S-$6.00   288-S-$5.00

289-S-$5.00   290-S-$5.00   291-S-$5.00   292-S-$5.00   293-S-$4.00   294-S-$5.00

295-$4.00   296-$5.00   297-Y-$5.00   298-$5.00   299-$5.00   300-$4.00

301-$5.00   303-$5.00

302-T-$25.00

304—M—$55.00

305—M—$100.00

306—M—$50.00

307—$45.00

308—$35.00

309—S—$35.00

310—$45.00

311—$12.00

312—$10.00

313—S—$20.00

314—$15.00

315—$15.00

316—S—$8.00

317—S—$8.00

318—S—$8.00

319—S—$8.00

320—O—$10.00

321—S—$15.00

322—S—$8.00

323—$8.00

324—$8.00

325—$8.00

326—S—$15.00

WILLIAM JENNINGS BRYAN 1896, 1900, 1908 CODE: BRY

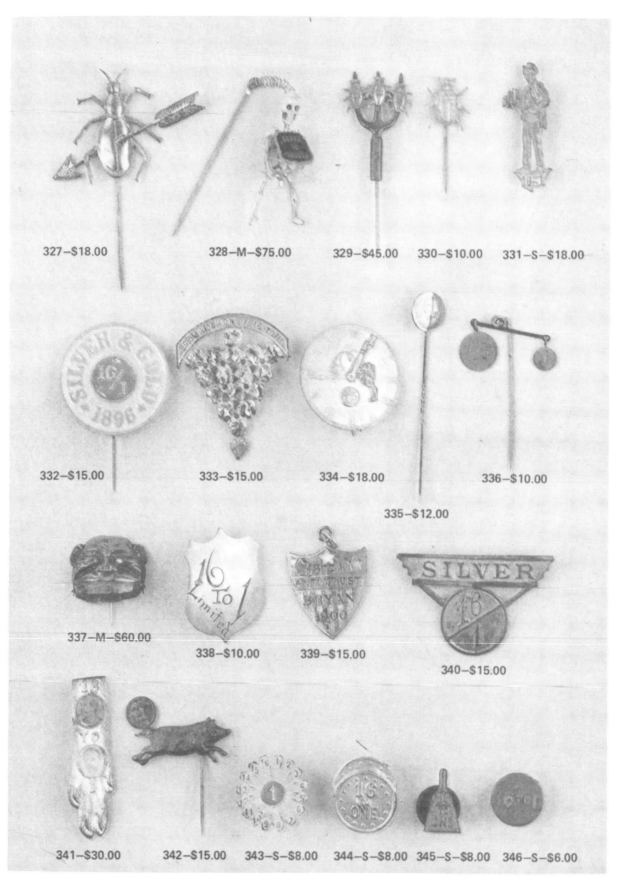

327—$18.00

328—M—$75.00

329—$45.00

330—$10.00

331—S—$18.00

332—$15.00

333—$15.00

334—$18.00

335—$12.00

336—$10.00

337—M—$60.00

338—$10.00

339—$15.00

340—$15.00

341—$30.00

342—$15.00

343—S—$8.00

344—S—$8.00

345—S—$8.00

346—S—$6.00

347—M—$30.00

348—$35.00

349—M—$55.00

350—$10.00

351—$15.00

352—$14.00

353—$18.00

354—M—$18.00

355—R—$7.00

356—$8.00

357—$12.00

358—$12.00

359—$10.00

360—$8.00

361—$100.00

362—$55.00

363—MN—$75.00

364—M $20.00

365—M—$15.00

366—$10.00 367—$8.00

368—$10.00

369—$25.00

370—M—$125.00

371—$12.00

372—$8.00 373—$14.00

374—MS—$15.00

375—$10.00 376—$10.00 377—$12.00 378—$10.00 379—$8.00

380—$12.00

381—$10.00

382—$12.00

383—$14.00

384—$12.00

385—$8.00

386—S—$5.00

387—$5.00

388—$6.00

389—S—$5.00

390—$8.00

391—$8.00

392—E—$12.00

393—$5.00

394—S—$10.00

395—S—$5.00

396—E—$6.00

397—E—$10.00

398—E—$8.00

399—E—$8.00

400—E—$6.00

401—E—$6.00

BRYAN ADDENDA

402–S–$15.00

403–S–$22.00

404–$12.00

405–$20.00

406–S–$15.00

407–$150.00

408–$100.00

409–A–$10.00

410–$15.00

411–$75.00

412–$135.00

413–$50.00

414–$15.00

415–$75.00

416–$40.00

417–$20.00

418–$20.00

419–$15.00

52

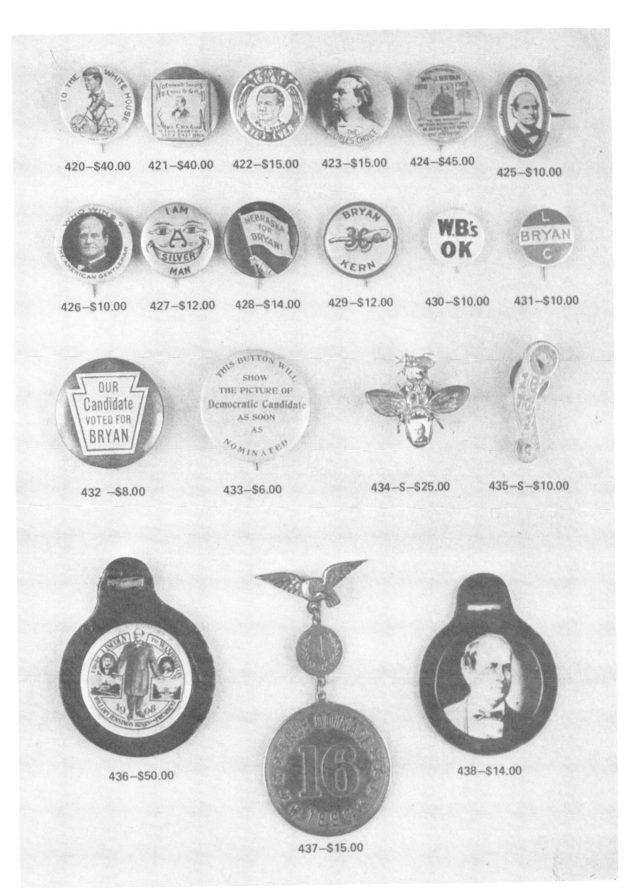

420—$40.00 421—$40.00 422—$15.00 423—$15.00 424—$45.00 425—$10.00

426—$10.00 427—$12.00 428—$14.00 429—$12.00 430—$10.00 431—$10.00

432 —$8.00 433—$6.00 434—S—$25.00 435—S—$10.00

436—$50.00 437—$15.00 438—$14.00

THEODORE ROOSEVELT — REPUBLICAN/PROGRESSIVE

Campaigns	1904	1912
	WON	LOST
Electoral Votes	336	88
Popular Votes	7,628,831	4,127,788
Running Mates	CHARLES W. FAIRBANKS	HIRAM W. JOHNSON
Conventions	CHICAGO	CHICAGO
Birth	NEW YORK, N.Y., OCT. 27, 1858	
Death	JAN. 6, 1919	

Theodore Roosevelt held numerous offices prior to the Spanish-American War, but it was his heroism as the leader of the "Rough Riders" that brought him great national popularity. New York Republican bosses selected him for the governorship which he won by a slim eighteen thousand votes. Roosevelt threw off the mantle of the bosses after assuming office in 1899 and made them anxious to be rid of him The solution was to exploit his popularity by running him as the Vice-Presidential candidate in 1900. McKinley, Mark Hanna and even Roosevelt himself disliked the idea, but Senator Thomas Platt, boss of New York State, organized a successful draft movement to nominate Roosevelt. Roosevelt added a comfortable margin to McKinley's second victory over Bryan, but Roosevelt felt his new job would be the end of his political career.

Mark Hanna had warned: "Don't any of you realize there's only one life between this madman and the White House?" Apparently the other powerful Republicans did not fear the worst, but it came to pass when McKinley was killed in Buffalo in 1901. Roosevelt assured Mark Hanna that he would continue McKinley's policies. Given Roosevelt's personality and the growing strength of the Progressive movement, it was inevitable that Roosevelt would chart his own course. Within six months Roosevelt moved against the trusts and went on to declare that it was his job "to see to it that every man has a square deal, no more and no less." There followed a series of domestic reforms and conservation measures that endeared him to the public. He obtained the 1904 nomination in spite of substantial party and big business opposition and went on to an easy victory over Alton B. Parker.

Having renounced a third term, Roosevelt helped nominate William Taft as his successor in 1908 and then departed for an African hunting trip. On his return he was unable to keep out of politics and became dissatisfied with his friend Taft. He decided on another run for the presidency in 1912, and when the Republicans gave Taft the nomination he bolted the party and became the candidate of the Progressive Party. During the campaign, Roosevelt was shot in Milwaukee and was saved only because the bullet hit his spectacle case and the speech folded in his breast pocket. In great pain, Roosevelt went on to finish his fifty minute address. Roosevelt got more votes than Taft, but the split in the Republican party gave the election to Wilson. There was discussion that Roosevelt might run again in 1916 and 1920, but neither possibility occurred and he died in January, 1919.

Roosevelt's strong personality still fascinates people and a number of collectors specialize in collecting his campaign items. There are a large number of single picture buttons in the five to ten dollar range. Buttons showing Roosevelt in his "Rough Rider" outfit with "Teddy" bears or a bull moose are especially popular. Jugates from 1912 of Roosevelt and Hiram Johnson are valued in excess of three hundred dollars.

1—$12.00

2—$14.00

3—$35.00

4—$18.00

5—$35.00

6—$14.00

7—$30.00

8—$22.00

9—$12.00

10—$30.00

11—$25.00

12—$35.00

13—$14.00

14—$20.00

15—$18.00

16—$25.00

17—$14.00

18—$14.00

19—$15.00

20—$18.00

21—$18.00

22—$14.00

23—$16.00

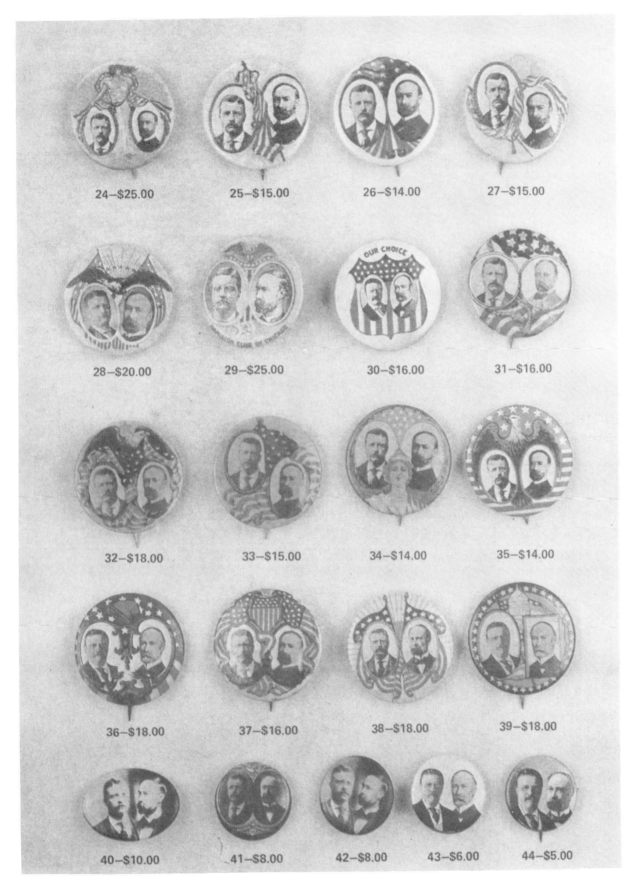

24—$25.00   25—$15.00   26—$14.00   27—$15.00

28—$20.00   29—$25.00   30—$16.00   31—$16.00

32—$18.00   33—$15.00   34—$14.00   35—$14.00

36—$18.00   37—$16.00   38—$18.00   39—$18.00

40—$10.00   41—$8.00   42—$8.00   43—$6.00   44—$5.00

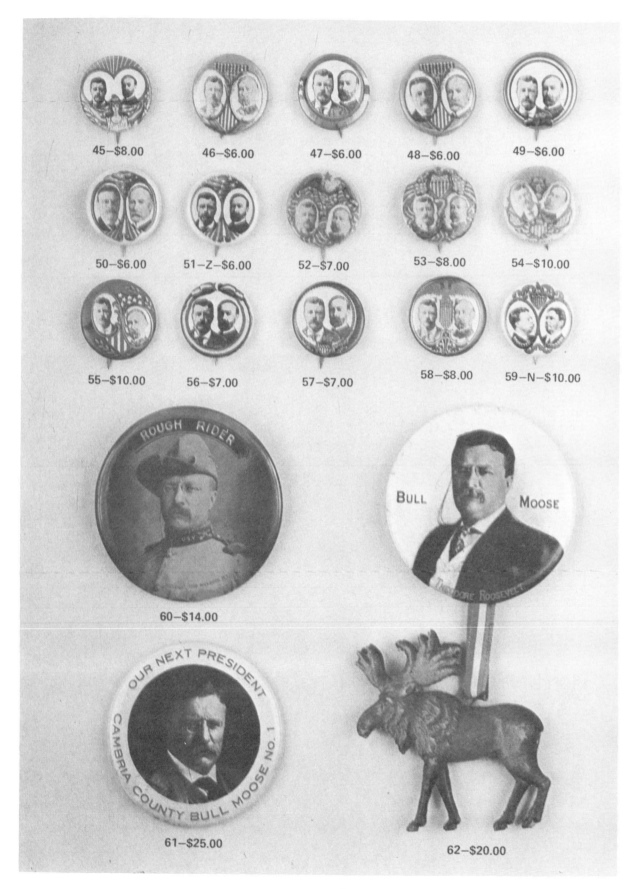

45—$8.00   46—$6.00   47—$6.00   48—$6.00   49—$6.00

50—$6.00   51—Z—$6.00   52—$7.00   53—$8.00   54—$10.00

55—$10.00   56—$7.00   57—$7.00   58—$8.00   59—N—$10.00

60—$14.00

61—$25.00   62—$20.00

THEODORE ROOSEVELT 1904, 1912 CODE: ROO

63—$18.00

64—$15.00

65—$14.00

66—$10.00

67—$30.00

68—$14.00

69—$16.00

70—$15.00

71—$25.00

72—$35.00

73—$25.00

74—$40.00

THEODORE ROOSEVELT 1904, 1912 CODE: ROO

75–$7.00   76–$5.00   77–$7.00   78–$6.00

79–$6.00   80–$10.00   81–$7.00   82–$6.00

83–$6.00   84–$6.00   85–$6.00   86–$35.00

87–$10.00   88–$10.00   89–$8.00   90–$8.00

91–$8.00   92–$7.00   93–$7.00   94–$7.00

95—Y—$20.00   96—$8.00   97—$7.00   98—$7.00

99—$8.00   100—$7.00   101—$7.00   102—$7.00

103—$7.00   104—$7.00   105—Y—$7.00   106—$8.00

107—$7.00   108—$6.00   109—$6.00   110—Z—$7.00

111—$7.00   112—$6.00   113—$6.00   114—$7.00

THEODORE ROOSEVELT 1904, 1912 CODE: ROO

115—$7.00   116—$7.00   117—$7.00   118—$7.00

119—$6.00   120—$6.00   121—$6.00   122—$6.00

123—$10.00   124—$15.00   125—$10.00   126—$10.00

127—$20.00   128—$5.00   129—$4.00   130—$4.00   131—$10.00

132—$10.00   133—$5.00   134—$8.00   135—$4.00   136—$4.00

137—$5.00   138—$4.00   139—$4.00   140—$4.00   141—$7.00

142—$6.00 143—$6.00 144—$6.00 145—$7.00 146—$5.00 147—$6.00

148—$10.00 149—$5.00 150—$5.00 151—$6.00 152—$5.00 153—$6.00

154—$10.00 155—$5.00 156—$6.00 157—$6.00 158—$6.00 159—$6.00

160—$7.00 161—$6.00 162—$10.00 163—$10.00 164—$10.00 165—$10.00

166—$5.00 167—$4.00 168—$6.00 169—$6.00 170—$7.00 171—$7.00

172—$7.00 173—$5.00 174—$25.00 175—$7.00 176—$12.00

177—$10.00 178—$8.00 179—$8.00 180—$8.00 181—$7.00

182—$12.00   183—$18.00   184—$12.00   185—$18.00   186—$10.00

187—N—$12.00   188—$10.00   189—$10.00   190—$12.00   191—$12.00

192—$125.00   193—$7.00   194—$7.00   195—$8.00

196—$15.00   197—$10.00   198—$5.00   199—$5.00   200—$5.00   201—$5.00

202—Y—$6.00   203—Y—$10.00   204—$6.00   205—$6.00   206—$6.00   207—$6.00

208—YZ—$4.00   209—$10.00   210—$6.00   211—$10.00

212—M—$60.00

213—M—$75.00

214—$30.00

215—$35.00

216—$15.00

217—$8.00

218—$15.00

219—$8.00

220—$10.00

221—M—$25.00

222—$25.00

223—H—$10.00

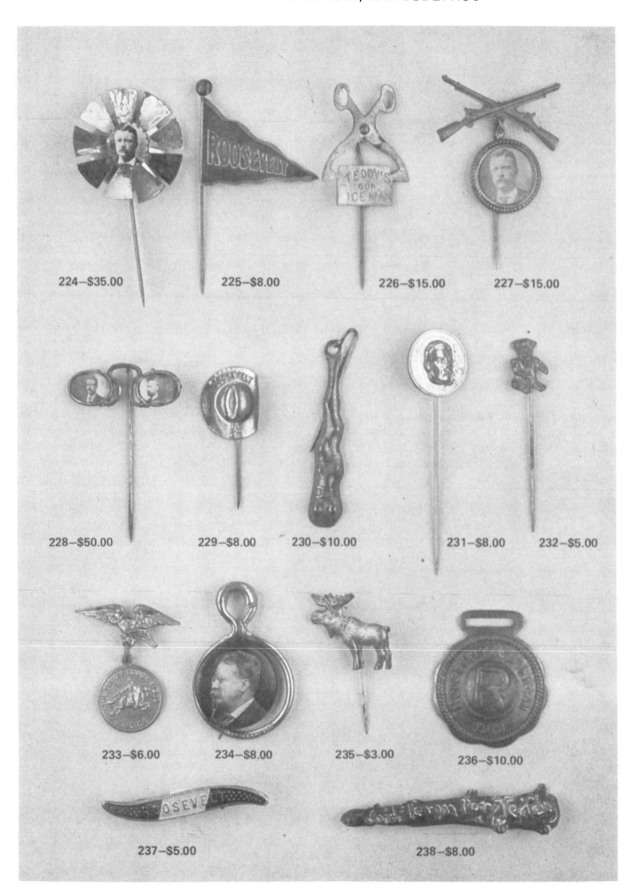

224—$35.00   225—$8.00   226—$15.00   227—$15.00

228—$50.00   229—$8.00   230—$10.00   231—$8.00   232—$5.00

233—$6.00   234—$8.00   235—$3.00   236—$10.00

237—$5.00   238—$8.00

THEODORE ROOSEVELT 1904, 1912 CODE: ROO

239—$15.00

240—$16.00

241—$16.00

242—U—$40.00

243—$10.00

244—$8.00

245—$6.00

246—LN—$8.00

247—$6.00

248—N—$6.00

249—$8.00

250—N—$6.00

251—$15.00

252—$35.00

253—$6.00

254—$135.00

255—$12.00

256—0—$8.00

257—$14.00

258—$18.00

259—$12.00

260—$20.00

261—$15.00

262—B—$50.00

263—$400.00

264—$350.00

265—$350.00

266—$30.00

267—$18.00

268—$18.00

269—$15.00

270—$100.00

271—$10.00

272—$12.00

273—$20.00

274—$10.00

275—$8.00

276—$8.00

277—$18.00

278—$28.00

279—$15.00

280—M—$25.00

281—$30.00

282—$25.00

283—$18.00

284—$18.00

285—$20.00

286—$15.00

ALTON B. PARKER — DEMOCRAT

Campaign	**1904**
	LOST
Electoral Votes	**140**
Popular Votes	**5,084,533**
Running Mate	**HENRY G. DAVIS**
Convention	**CHICAGO**
Birth	**CORTLAND, N.Y., MAY 14, 1852**
Death	**MAY 10, 1926**

Alton B. Parker was a New York judge nominated by the Democrats in 1904 as a "safe and sane" candidate. This was after the Eastern Democrats regained control from the Western and Southern elements that had given William Jennings Bryan two tries at the presidency. It was hoped that Judge Parker, with something of a reputation as a conservative Democrat, would rally the Republican businessmen disenchanted with Roosevelt's policies. An eighty-one year old West Virginia millionaire, Henry G. Davis, was selected for Vice-President with the expectation he would make a substantial financial contribution to the campaign fund. This was an idle hope.

The convention wished to remain silent on the gold and silver issue, but Parker insisted on endorsing the gold standard as now firmly established and the party leaders accepted his position. There was little in the way of new campaign issues, and the business community preferred the impulsive Republican Roosevelt to the conservative Democrat Parker.

Roosevelt won by a great majority as Parker failed to carry a single state north of the Mason and Dixon line. Roosevelt promptly issued his declaration that he would not accept the nomination in 1908, a statement he came to regret.

The buttons for Alton B. Parker reflect the lack of campaign issues in 1904. The overwhelming majority of buttons simply show Parker's picture. However, Parker's buttons are noted for their exceptionally bright colors and intricate graphic designs which makes them a favorite with collectors. One of the very rare Parker buttons implied that Roosevelt favored intermarriage of blacks and whites. Under a small picture of Parker appeared another picture of a white bride and groom while under Roosevelt's picture is another picture of a black groom beside a white bride. The slogan was "It's Up to You — Take Your Choice." This button was probably inspired by the fact that Roosevelt was the first President to invite a black man, Booker T. Washington, to dine at the White House. A pro-Roosevelt button showed Roosevelt and Washington seated and dining together beneath the word "Equality" around the top edge of the button.

Most Parker single picture buttons sell for ten to fifteen dollars, and the range for jugates is from ten to twenty-five dollars. As there were no heated issues in the 1904 campaign, very little in the way of satirical or novelty items was produced.

1—$35.00

2—$30.00

3—$30.00

4—$25.00

5—$30.00

6—$18.00

7—$30.00

8—$25.00

9—$30.00

10—$20.00

11—$25.00

12—$35.00

13—$20.00

ALTON B. PARKER 1904 CODE: PAR

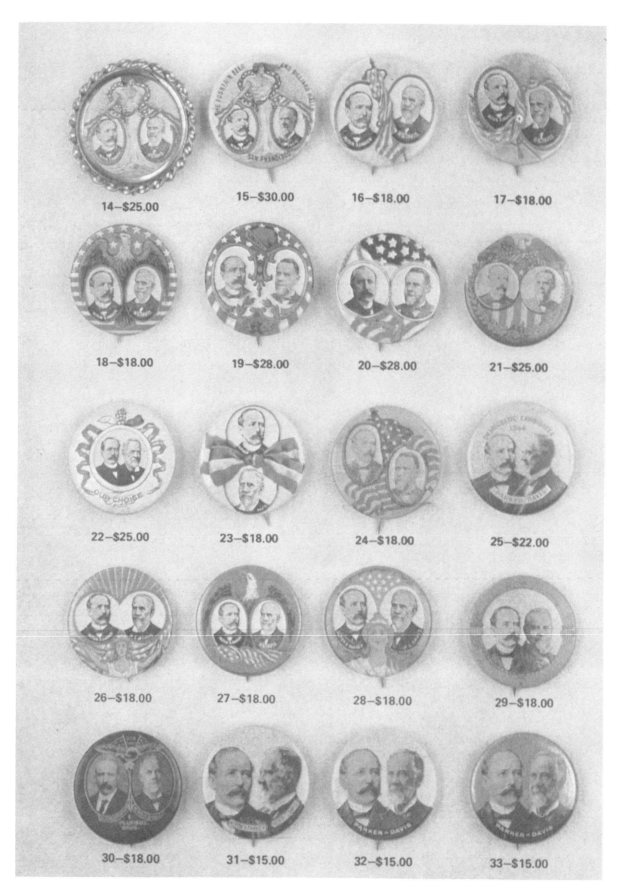

14—$25.00

15—$30.00

16—$18.00

17—$18.00

18—$18.00

19—$28.00

20—$28.00

21—$25.00

22—$25.00

23—$18.00

24—$18.00

25—$22.00

26—$18.00

27—$18.00

28—$18.00

29—$18.00

30—$18.00

31—$15.00

32—$15.00

33—$15.00

ALTON B. PARKER 1904 CODE: PAR

34—$15.00   35—$14.00   36—$14.00   37—$14.00   38—$12.00   39—$14.00

40—$12.00   41—$15.00   42—$15.00   43—$12.00   44—$12.00   45—$12.00

46—$14.00   47—$14.00   48—$12.00   49—$15.00   50—X—$12.00   51—$12.00

52—$15.00   53—$15.00   54—$14.00

55—$14.00   56—$18.00   57—$12.00

ALTON B. PARKER 1904 CODE: PAR

58—$12.00

59—$10.00

60—$10.00

61—$10.00

62—$10.00

FOR PRESIDENT

63—$12.00

64—$15.00

65—$14.00

66—$14.00

67—$18.00

68—$10.00

69—$8.00

70—$8.00

71—$10.00

72—$22.00

74

73—$12.00

74—$10.00

75—$12.00

76—$12.00

77—$8.00

78—$10.00

79—$10.00

80—$12.00

81—$10.00

82—$10.00

83—$10.00

84—$10.00

85—$12.00

86—$10.00

87—$10.00

88—$10.00

89—$10.00

90—$10.00

91—$12.00

92—$10.00

ALTON B. PARKER 1904 CODE: PAR

93—$6.00 94—$8.00 95—$6.00 96—$6.00 97—$6.00 98—$6.00

99—$6.00 100—$6.00 101—$6.00 102—$8.00 103—$8.00 104—$6.00

105—$8.00 106—$6.00 107—$8.00 108—$6.00 109—$6.00 110—$18.00

111—$12.00 112—Y—$40.00 113—$8.00 114—$8.00

115—$12.00 116—$8.00 117—$10.00 118—$10.00

119—$12.00

120—$20.00

121—$8.00

122—$14.00

123—$20.00

PARKER   DAVIS

124—$15.00

PARKER ADDENDA

125—$35.00

126—S—$20.00

127—$15.00

128—$15.00

129—$22.00

130—$20.00

131—$22.00

132—$14.00

133—$15.00

134—$10.00

135—$55.00

136—$12.00

WILLIAM HOWARD TAFT — REPUBLICAN

Campaigns	1908	1912
	WON	LOST
Electoral Votes	321	8
Popular Votes	7,679,114	3,485,831
Running Mates	JAMES S. SHERMAN	JAMES S. SHERMAN
Conventions	CHICAGO	CHICAGO
Birth	CINCINNATI, OHIO, SEPT. 15, 1857	
Death	MARCH 8, 1930	

William Howard Taft was the natural choice of Theodore Roosevelt to carry the Republican banner in 1908. Their friendship was long established and close. Although Taft would have preferred to become Chief Justice of the Supreme Court, the position was not open at the time and he decided to announce his availability for the nomination.

Taft had been appointed by McKinley in 1900 as the first governor of the Philippine Islands. Although opposed to annexation, Taft believed the Filipinos needed to be taught self-government before acquiring independence. He dedicated himself to this task and later turned down two separate offers from Roosevelt of a seat on the Supreme Court. By 1903, Roosevelt offered Taft the position of Secretary of War and Taft was ready to come home. He was very successful in the position and Roosevelt came to rely on his assistance. In 1906, another Court vacancy tempted Taft but pressure from his wife and brother convinced him to wait for the presidential nomination.

Taft was nominated on the first ballot and went on to defeat Bryan by a million votes. Roosevelt expected Taft to advance his progressive policies, but Taft recognized he was best suited to perfecting the legal machinery needed to firmly establish Roosevelt's advances rather than making bold new policies on his own. This gave Taft's administration the appearance of moving much slower than Roosevelt's administration.

When Roosevelt returned from an African hunting trip his natural energy led him back into politics. His views were more progressive than ever and he began attacks, often unwarranted, on his old friend Taft who refrained from defending himself. Eventually, as Roosevelt became more aggressive, Taft came to consider him radical and socialistic and decided upon running for re-election. Taft managed to win the nomination in 1912, but Roosevelt bolted the party and the split gave the election to Wilson.

Taft returned to private life but was called back to public service by Wilson. Finally, in 1921, President Harding gave Taft what he had wanted for so long — the Chief Justiceship of the Supreme Court. He held the position for nine happy years until a heart ailment forced his retirement in 1930 and he died a month later.

Although many of Taft's buttons are colorful and well designed, very few reflect the issues of the times. A strong art nouveau influence is found in the graphics on some well designed buttons. There are a wide variety of jugates and the 1¼" size is rarer than the 7/8" size.

1—$75.00

2—$25.00

3—$50.00

4—$60.00

5—M—$60.00

6—$55.00

7—$100.00

8—$45.00

9—$35.00

10—$22.00

11—$25.00

12—$27.00

13—$25.00

14—N—$25.00

15–L–$30.00

16–$10.00

17–$18.00

18–$15.00

19–$18.00

20–$25.00

21–$18.00

22–$20.00

23–$18.00

24–$18.00

25–$20.00

26–$25.00

27–$15.00

28–$15.00

29–$25.00

WILLIAM HOWARD TAFT 1908, 1912 CODE: TAF

30—$20.00   31—$22.00   32—Y—$20.00   33—$25.00

34—NY—$12.00 35—Z—$7.00 36—$6.00 37—$6.00 38—$8.00 39—$8.00

40—$12.00 41—$10.00 42—$10.00 43—$10.00 44—$12.00 45—$10.00

46—$30.00

WILLIAM HOWARD TAFT 1908, 1912 CODE: TAF

47—$20.00

48—$12.00

49—$40.00

50—$12.00

51—Y—$10.00

52—$12.00

53—$10.00

54—$10.00

55—$10.00

56—$10.00

57—$8.00

58—$8.00

59—$8.00

60—$8.00

61—$8.00

62—$10.00

63—$8.00

64—$8.00

65—$8.00

WILLIAM HOWARD TAFT 1908, 1912 CODE: TAF

66—$15.00   67—$15.00   68—$12.00   69—$12.00

70—$8.00   71—$8.00   72—$10.00   73—$8.00

74—$5.00   75—$5.00   76—$8.00   77—$8.00

78—$6.00   79—$6.00   80—$6.00   81—$6.00

82—$6.00   83—$6.00   84—$6.00   85—$6.00

86—$8.00   87—$8.00   88—$8.00   89—$8.00

90—$12.00   91—$10.00   92—$8.00   93—$8.00

94—$8.00   95—$8.00   96—L—$8.00   97—$12.00

98—$25.00   99—$8.00   100—$6.00   101—$6.00   102—$6.00   103—$6.00

104—$6.00   105—$6.00   106—$6.00   107—$8.00   108—$8.00   109—$6.00

110—$8.00   111—$8.00   112—$8.00   113—$6.00   114—$8.00   115—$8.00

WILLIAM HOWARD TAFT 1908, 1912 CODE: TAF

116—$8.00 117—$6.00 118—$6.00 119—$6.00 120—$8.00 121—$10.00

122—$8.00 123—$8.00 124—$5.00 125—$5.00 126—$6.00 127—$6.00

128—$6.00 129—$6.00 130—$12.00 131—$6.00 132—$6.00 133—$6.00

134—$6.00 135—$6.00 136—$6.00 137—$6.00 138—$6.00 139—$6.00

140—$6.00 141—$5.00 142—$12.00 143—$4.00 144—$4.00 145—$8.00

146—DN—$6.00 147—$6.00 148—$6.00 149—$8.00 150—$5.00 151—$5.00

152—$3.00 153—$3.00 154—$3.00 155—$3.00 156—$4.00 157—$3.00

158—$7.00   159—$4.00   160—$3.00   161—$5.00   162—$3.00   163—$3.00

164—$30.00   165—$15.00   166—$8.00   167—$8.00

169—$15.00

168—R—$22.00

170—R—$5.00   171—$4.00   172—$4.00   173—$5.00

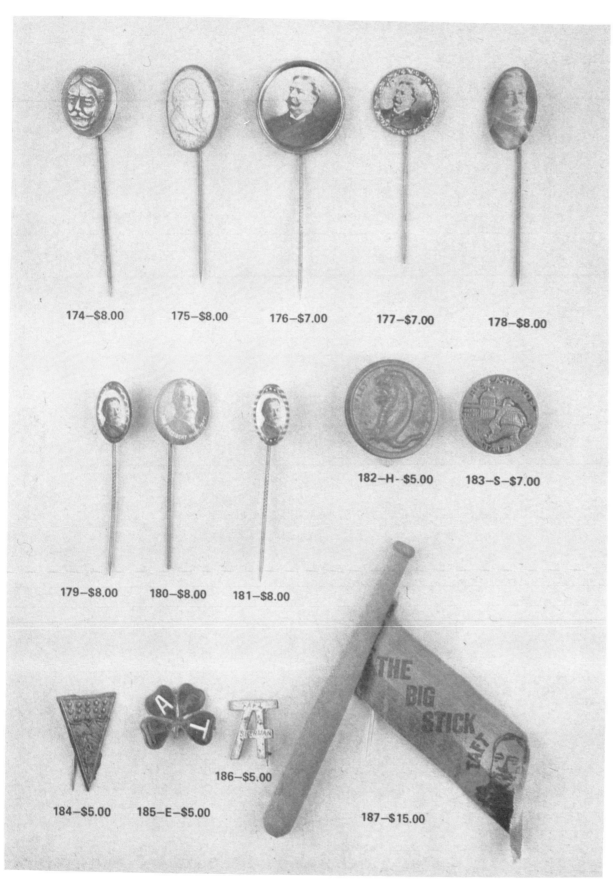

174—$8.00   175—$8.00   176—$7.00   177—$7.00   178—$8.00

179—$8.00   180—$8.00   181—$8.00

182—H—$5.00   183—S—$7.00

184—$5.00   185—E—$5.00   186—$5.00   187—$15.00

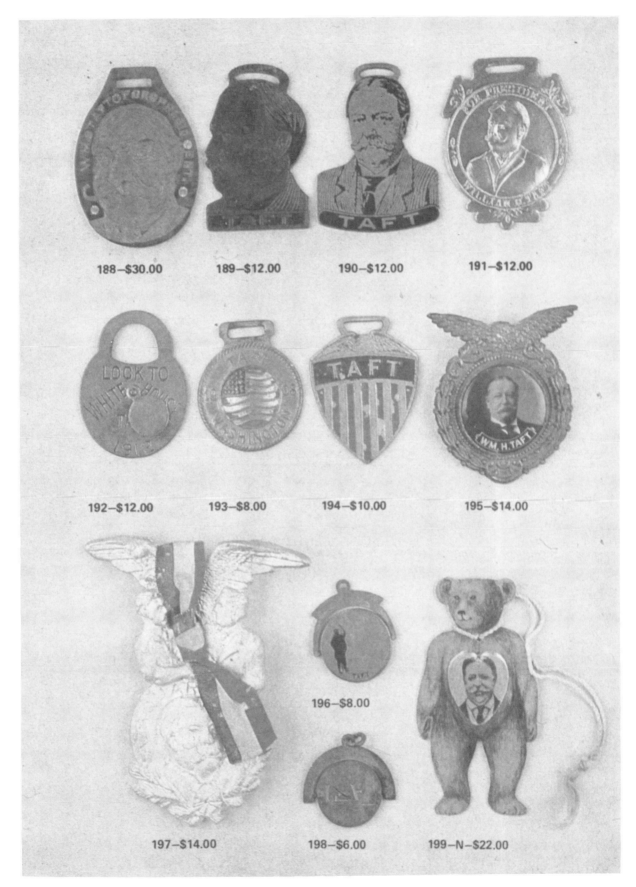

188—$30.00   189—$12.00   190—$12.00   191—$12.00

192—$12.00   193—$8.00   194—$10.00   195—$14.00

197—$14.00

196—$8.00

198—$6.00

199—N—$22.00

200—$14.00

201—$14.00

202—$14.00

203—$125.00

204—$25.00

205-1—$28.00

IT'S UP TO THE MAN ON THE OTHER SIDE TO PUT THIS TRIED & SAFE MAN AT THE HEAD OF THE GOVERNMENT

206—$15.00

207—$15.00

208—$12.00

209—$12.00

210-M—$65.00

211—$40.00

212—$12.00

213—$7.00

214—$8.00

215—$12.00

WOODROW WILSON – DEMOCRAT

Campaigns	1912	1916
	WON	WON
Electoral Votes	435	277
Popular Votes	6,301,254	9,131,511
Running Mates	THOMAS R. MARSHALL	THOMAS R. MARSHALL
Conventions	BALTIMORE	ST. LOUIS
Birth	STAUNTON, VA., DEC. 28, 1856	
Death	FEB. 3, 1924	

Woodrow Wilson became New Jersey's progressive governor in 1910, after a career as a college professor and President of Princeton University. At the Baltimore convention in 1912, Champ Clark, Speaker of the House, led in the balloting but could not get the necessary two-thirds vote required for nomination. William Jennings Bryan, during the fourteenth ballot, announced he would not give his support to anyone who had the support of Tammany. This improved Wilson's position and his nomination finally came on the forty-sixth ballot.

Wilson's policies were known as "New Freedom" and resembled Roosevelt's policies, but both were more progressive than Taft. Wilson's victory was no surprise with the Republicans split between Taft and Roosevelt and he won forty states to become the first Democratic President since Grover Cleveland. During his first term Wilson enacted a child labor law and secured passage of eight hour day legislation. As his administration progressed, public attention came to focus more and more on the war between Germany and England.

The English passenger liner Lusitania was sunk by a German submarine in May, 1915, with a loss of one hundred twenty-four Americans. Wilson resisted pressure to declare war immediately and tried instead to issue firm warnings to the Germans. By 1916, however, he agreed to a program of military preparedness.

The Democratic convention was solidly behind Wilson and he was praised, more than he wanted to be, as "the man who kept us out of war." Charles E. Hughes, with Roosevelt's support, campaigned energetically against Wilson and on election day was the apparent winner. By the next morning it was discovered that Hughes was still uncertain of California and its thirteen electoral votes he needed to win. When all the votes were counted, Wilson was the winner by four thousand votes and thus carried the state and the election.

By 1917, America was into the war. After the armistice, Wilson spent his remaining time in office making a valiant but unsuccessful effort to convince Congress to join his beloved League of Nations. Wilson finished his term bedridden, partially paralyzed, and mentally exhausted.

By 1912 and 1916 fewer buttons were being issued in bright colors and with intricate designs. Most jugates and single picture buttons in the 7/8" size sell for ten to twenty dollars. Jugates in the 1¼" size are particularly scarce and most sell for one hundred dollars or more.

1—$100.00   2—$75.00   3—$100.00   4—$100.00

5—$60.00   6—$75.00   7—$100.00   8—$85.00

9—$12.00   10—$12.00   11—Z—$12.00   12—$12.00   13—Z—$12.00   14—$14.00

15—$20.00   16—$25.00   17—$14.00   18—$18.00   19—$25.00   20—$10.00

21—Z—$90.00   22—$20.00   23—$14.00

24—$22.00

25—$18.00

26—$14.00

27—$15.00

28—Z—$65.00

29—$18.00

30—$18.00

31—$18.00

32—$8.00

33—$8.00

34—$10.00

35—$6.00

36—$28.00

37—$18.00

38—$20.00

39—$15.00

40—$20.00

41—$18.00

42—$18.00

43—L—$18.00

44—$10.00   45—$8.00   46—$8.00   47—$8.00   48—$8.00   49—$12.00

50—$14.00   51—$8.00   52—Z—$6.00   53—$10.00   54—$8.00   55—$8.00

56—$8.00   57—$6.00   58—Z—$6.00   59—Z—$6.00   60—$8.00   61—$12.00

62—$8.00   63—$10.00   64—$10.00   65—$10.00   66—$8.00   67—$8.00

68—$8.00   69—$8.00   70—$8.00   71—$8.00   72—$8.00   73—$8.00

74—$12.00   75—$8.00   76—$8.00   77—$12.00   78—$8.00   79—$8.00

80—$6.00   81—$6.00   82—$5.00   83—$5.00   84—$5.00   85—S—$6.00

86—$75.00

87—$75.00

88—$15.00

89—$12.00

90—$25.00

91—$20.00

92—$18.00

93—$10.00

94—$12.00

95—$12.00

96—$12.00

97—$12.00

98—$14.00

99—$12.00

100—Y—$6.00

101—$7.00

102—$7.00

103—$7.00

104—$6.00

105—$8.00

106—Y—$7.00

107—$7.00

108—$4.00

109—$4.00

110—$5.00

111—$5.00

112—$4.00

113—$4.00

114—$3.00

115—$4.00

116—$3.00

117—$14.00

118—$14.00

119—$15.00

120—$14.00

121—$7.00

122—$5.00

123—$8.00   124—$10.00   125—$10.00   126—$6.00   127—$6.00

128—$10.00   129—$8.00   130—$8.00   131—$10.00   132—$10.00   133—$8.00

134—$125.00

135—$110.00

136—$100.00

137—$100.00

138—$60.00

139—$100.00

140—$100.00

141—$12.00

142—$12.00

143—$14.00

144—$12.00

145—$50.00

146—$20.00

147—$50.00

148—$35.00

149—$15.00

150—$18.00

151—$15.00

CHARLES EVANS HUGHES — REPUBLICAN

Campaign	**1916**
	LOST
Electoral Votes	**254**
Popular Votes	**8,548,935**
Running Mate	**CHARLES W. FAIRBANKS**
Convention	**CHICAGO**
Birth	**GLENS FALLS, N.Y. APRIL 11, 1862**
Death	**AUG. 27, 1948**

In 1916, the Republicans were determined to heal the party split that cost them the election in 1912. Charles Evans Hughes, an Associate Justice of the Supreme Court and former Governor of New York, seemed to be the best man. His record as Governor was acceptable to the Progressives and his Supreme Court decisions satisfied the conservative Republicans. The Progressives did meet and nominated Theodore Roosevelt, but he declined the nomination with the reservation that he might change his mind if the Republican platform failed to take a firm stand on the war issue. Later, Roosevelt endorsed Hughes and this brought an end to the Progressive Party as there was no longer much difference between their platform and the Republican platform

Hughes campaigned hard but did not arouse the electorate. The war was the overriding issue and the Democratic campaign slogan that Wilson "kept us out of war" was difficult to attack. On a campaign trip in California, Hughes was ushered around by William H. Croker, a conservative national committeeman who still opposed the state's Progressive Governor Hiram W. Johnson. Hughes could have had Johnson's endorsement, but was prevented from meeting him even though they both were staying in the same hotel. Hughes went on to lose California by less than four thousand votes while Johnson, running for the Senate, won by three hundred thousand votes. Hughes later became Warren Harding's Secretary of State and ended his career as Chief Justice of the Supreme Court.

Aside from a few picture and name buttons, most Hughes items are rather scarce. Particularly rare are 1¼" jugates. There are very few buttons that reflect the issues of 1916. One lithographed tin button was designed in 1916 for both Hughes and Wilson. It shows the candidate's picture and name against a background of red, white and blue stars and stripes. Lithographed tin buttons did not become common until the 1920 election. Most Hughes single picture buttons sell for over fifteen dollars and jugates are rarely found for less than thirty dollars.

1—$100.00

2—$65.00

3—$35.00

4—$35.00

5—$35.00

6—U—$45.00

7—U—$18.00

8—$20.00

9—$20.00

10—L—$20.00

11—$20.00

12—$22.00

13—$15.00

14—$10.00

15—$10.00

16—$8.00

17—$10.00

18—$8.00

19—$12.00

20—$14.00

21—Z—$12.00

22—$15.00

23—$7.00

24—$7.00

25—$7.00

26—$12.00   27—$8.00   28—$12.00   29—$12.00   30—$6.00   31—$7.00

33—$10.00   34—$6.00   35—$8.00   36—$6.00   37—$10.00

32—$12.00

38—$6.00   39—$8.00   40—$10.00   41—$8.00   42—$7.00   43—$8.00

44—$4.00   45—$4.00   46—$4.00   47—$4.00   48—$4.00   49—$4.00

50—$4.00   51—L—$3.00   52—$3.00   53—$3.00   54—S—$4.00   55—S—$5.00

56—$20.00   57—$14.00

58—$125.00

59—$125.00

60—$125.00

61—$35.00

62—$4.00

63—$40.00

64—$35.00

65—$25.00

66—$25.00

67—$25.00

68—$30.00

69—$12.00

70—$12.00

71—$12.00

72—$10.00

73—$7.00

74–L—$25.00

75—$10.00

WARREN G. HARDING — REPUBLICAN

Campaign	1920
	WON
Electoral Votes	404
Popular Votes	16,153,115
Running Mate	CALVIN COOLIDGE
Convention	CHICAGO
Birth	BLOOMING GROVE, OHIO, NOV. 2, 1865
Death	AUG. 2, 1923

The Republicans had many candidates to choose from in 1920. The convention became deadlocked by the two front runners, General Leonard Wood and Governor Frank O. Lowden. The solution came in the famous "smoke-filled room" where dark horse candidate Warren G. Harding was selected for the nomination by the party bosses. For Vice-President the bosses wanted Senator Irvine Lenroot of Wisconsin, but the delegates rebelled and nominated Massachusetts Governor Calvin Coolidge who had gained national prominence by breaking the Boston police strike in 1919.

Even Harding was surprised by the nomination. His Senatorial career had been decidedly lackluster and a few days before the nomination had said privately that he was quitting politics. However, Harding had qualities attractive to the Republican leaders. Aside from his good looks, Harding was unprincipled, pliable, and favored business unfettered by governmental regulations.

A few weeks before his nomination, Harding had said: "America's present need is not for heroics but healing; not for nostrums but normalcy; not revolution but restoration." Normalcy became the recurrent theme of his campaign.

Harding decided on a "front-porch campaign" in the style of William McKinley and received his visitors at home. The campaign developed little enthusiasm and only half the eligible voters cast their ballots. Harding's overwhelming victory of four hundred and four electoral votes to one hundred twenty-seven for James Cox was also a final defeat for Woodrow Wilson who had maintained the principles and League of Nations he fought for would be vindicated by the voters.

The 1920 election was the first that women could vote in and Harding was the first President to ride an automobile in his inauguration parade. In 1923, on a return trip from a visit to Alaska, Harding received a coded message from Washington that further upset his already precarious physical condition. At San Francisco he was taken to the Palace Hotel. Physicians described his condition as grave and he died five days later. The cause of death went undetermined as Mrs. Harding refused to permit an autopsy. At first Harding was mourned, but six months later a flood of persistent rumors about corruption in high places became confirmed with the exposure of the Teapot Dome oil scandals.

Fewer varieties of campaign items were issued in 1920 than in any previous election since 1896. There are a few common Harding picture buttons and lithographed tin name buttons, but most Harding buttons are scarce. Harding and Coolidge jugates are extremely rare and less than ten design varieties are known.

1—$450.00

2—$400.00

3—$350.00

4—$400.00

5—$35.00

6—$35.00

7—$35.00

8—$30.00

9—$30.00

10-Z—$35.00

11—$35.00

12—$35.00

13—$12.00

14-YZ—$5.00

15-Y—$5.00

16-YZ—$5.00

17—$5.00

18—$12.00

19—$15.00

20—$12.00

21—$14.00

22—$14.00

23—$10.00

24—$10.00

25—$400.00

26—$300.00

27—$325.00

28—$400.00

29—$40.00

30—I—$55.00

31—$35.00

32—$20.00

33—$20.00

34—$20.00

35—$12.00

36—$30.00

37—$6.00

38—$8.00

39—$10.00

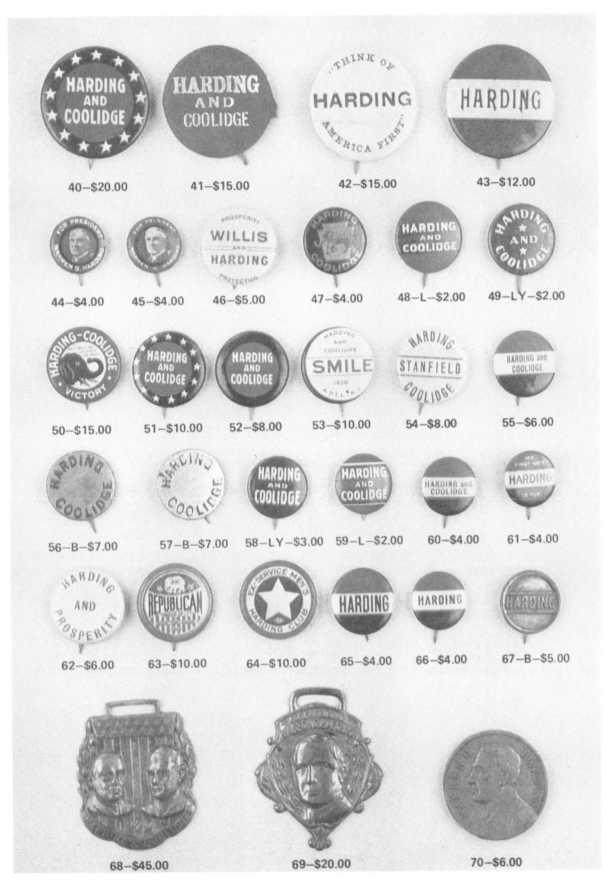

40—$20.00   41—$15.00   42—$15.00   43—$12.00

44—$4.00   45—$4.00   46—$5.00   47—$4.00   48—L—$2.00   49—LY—$2.00

50—$15.00   51—$10.00   52—$8.00   53—$10.00   54—$8.00   55—$6.00

56—B—$7.00   57—B—$7.00   58—LY—$3.00   59—L—$2.00   60—$4.00   61—$4.00

62—$6.00   63—$10.00   64—$10.00   65—$4.00   66—$4.00   67—B—$5.00

68—$45.00   69—$20.00   70—$6.00

71—$35.00

UNDER
The 19th
Amendment
I Cast My
FIRST VOTE
Nov. 2nd, 1920

72—$15.00

WOMEN'S
FIRST VOTE
—
VOTE
THE
STRAIGHT
REPUBLICAN
TICKET

73—$8.00

DON'T THROW YOUR VOTE AWAY
PUT IT IN THIS TRUNK

74—M—$25.00   75—C—$10.00

76—S—$3.00   77—E—$10.00   78—E—$10.00

79—S—$5.00   80—SE—$6.00   81—SE—$6.00   82—SE—$5.00

HARDING

83—$5.00   84—$4.00

85—$6.00   86—$5.00

87—$15.00

JAMES M. COX – DEMOCRAT

Campaign	1920
	LOST
Electoral Votes	127
Popular Votes	9,133,092
Running Mate	FRANKLIN DELANO ROOSEVELT
Convention	SAN FRANCISCO
Birth	JACKSONBURG, OHIO, MARCH 31, 1870
Death	JULY 15, 1957

Governor James Cox shared a few similarities with his opponent Warren G. Harding. Both were from Ohio, both had risen in newspaper publishing, and both were little known outside their state. Cox, however, was unimpressive compared to the handsome Harding and he was cast in the mold of the progressive Wilsonian tradition. Cox, like Harding, became a compromise candidate at the party convention. After a stand-off between William McAdoo, Wilson's son-in-law, and Attorney General A. Palmer Mitchell, Cox got the nomination on the forty-fourth ballot. Cox chose as his running mate Franklin Delano Roosevelt, a handsome young New Yorker with an impressive record as the Assistant Secretary of the Navy.

Cox stood by Wilson's record and favored entry into the League of Nations. He traveled tirelessly and set a record of visiting eighteen states on a twenty-nine day Western swing. His efforts were futile as voters were ready to endorse Harding and his return to "normalcy." As a footnote, Eugene V. Debs, Socialist candidate for President, received nearly a million votes although he was in a Federal prison during the entire campaign convicted of sedition. One rare button shows Debs in his convict uniform and reads "For President Convict No. 9653."

The Democrats issued very few campaign items in 1920. A white metal rooster issued for Cox is the most commonly found item. A few lithographed tin name buttons are the next most common items, but all picture buttons of Cox are rare.

The Cox and Roosevelt jugate is the most highly valued of all campaign buttons, although with approximately fifty specimens known it is certainly not the rarest button. A Cox and Roosevelt jugate pocketwatch and a brass jugate watch fob were issued. A quantity of the jugate watch fobs, along with a matching Harding and Coolidge jugate fob, were discovered several years ago.

By 1920, truly colorful and intricately designed buttons were seldom manufactured. The vast majority of presidential campaign buttons issued after 1916 were colored sepia, black and white, or red, white and blue. Lithographed tin buttons were widely introduced in 1920 and become increasingly common thereafter because they cost less to produce than celluloid buttons.

JAMES M. COX 1920 CODE: COX

1–N–$2,000.00   2–$125.00   3–$100.00   4–$100.00   5–$100.00

6–$50.00   7–$85.00   8–$75.00

9–$85.00   10–$85.00   11–$80.00   12–$80.00   13–$95.00

14–$85.00   15–$85.00   16–Z–$85.00   17–$75.00   18–$25.00   19–$50.00

20–$25.00   21–$25.00   22–B–$25.00   23–B–$25.00   24–$25.00   25–Z–$25.00   26–$25.00

27–L–$18.00   29–LY–$17.00
28–L–$17.00   30–$18.00   31–$18.00   32–L–$18.00   33–L–$18.00

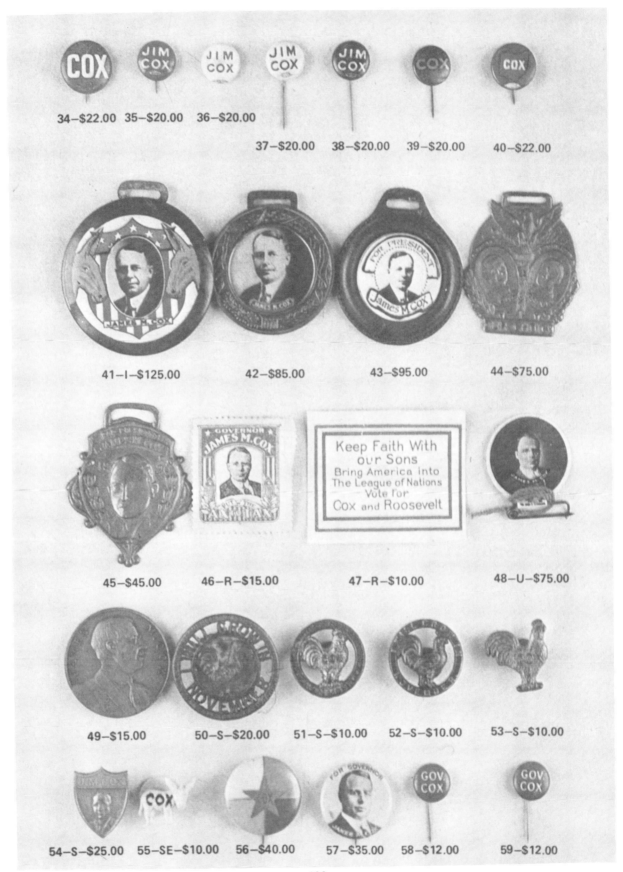

34—$22.00 35—$20.00 36—$20.00

37—$20.00 38—$20.00 39—$20.00 40—$22.00

41—I—$125.00 42—$85.00 43—$95.00 44—$75.00

45—$45.00 46—R—$15.00 47—R—$10.00 48—U—$75.00

Keep Faith With
our Sons
Bring America into
The League of Nations
Vote for
Cox and Roosevelt

49—$15.00 50—S—$20.00 51—S—$10.00 52—S—$10.00 53—S—$10.00

54—S—$25.00 55—SE—$10.00 56—$40.00 57—$35.00 58—$12.00 59—$12.00

CALVIN COOLIDGE — REPUBLICAN

Campaign	**1924**
	WON
Electoral Votes	**382**
Popular Votes	**15,719,921**
Running Mate	**CHARLES G. DAWES**
Convention	**CLEVELAND**
Birth	**PLYMOUTH NOTCH, VT., JULY 4, 1872**
Death	**JAN. 5, 1933**

Calvin Coolidge was chosen as Harding's running mate in 1920 because of the national prominence he gained in settling the Boston police strike of 1919. As a Vice-President he made few contributions and avoided all confrontations. There was even a chance the Republicans would drop him from the ticket in 1924, but Harding's death made Coolidge President on August 2, 1923.

Coolidge, a conservative New Englander, was ideal to carry on Harding's program of "normalcy." He even managed to maintain public confidence in himself during the Teapot Dome scandals which disgraced many of Harding's appointees still in the government. As Democrats tried to implicate Coolidge, he remained aloof and restrained. The Republican leaders began to rally around him and decided his nomination in 1924 would demonstrate the corruption was attributable to individuals and not the party.

Charles G. Dawes, a former Chicago banker, became his running mate and the two won an easy victory over Democrat John Davis and Progressive Robert M. LaFollette.

"Coolidge prosperity" was based on an overheated stock market. Occasional tremors were calmed by public reassurances offered by Coolidge and Andrew Mellon, his Secretary of the Treasury. Coolidge maintained that regulation of the New York Stock Exchange should be handled by the state and not the federal government.

On August 2, 1927, after four years in office, Coolidge announced, "I do not choose to run for President in 1928." He felt ten years in office would be too long, but also his wife remarked that he had said a depression was coming. Coolidge recognized the time was at hand for government to be more aggressive, but did not see himself as the man to effect the changes. After leaving office he retired to New England, where he carefully guarded his privacy until he died.

As in 1920, relatively few varieties of buttons were issued. The Republicans continued to issue more varieties of campaign items than the Democrats, but the number is small compared to the profusion of the early 1900's. Any Coolidge jugates larger than 1" are very rare.

1—$175.00

2—$350.00

3—Z—$125.00

4—S—$50.00

5—$50.00

6—YZ—$10.00

7—$30.00

8—L—$75.00

9—L—$75.00

10—$40.00

11—Y—$45.00

12—$35.00

13—$30.00

14—$30.00

15—$35.00

16—$15.00

17—$35.00

18—$20.00

19—$15.00

20—$15.00

21—$10.00

22—$350.00

23—$350.00

OUR PRESIDENT
DEEDS - NOT WORDS

25—$60.00

24—$45.00

26—$35.00

27—$35.00

VOTERS OF THE U.S.A.

KEEP COOL-IDGE
LESS TAXES - LARGER SERVICE
BALANCED BUSINESS

28—$35.00

29—$12.00

30—A—$40.00

31—$4.00

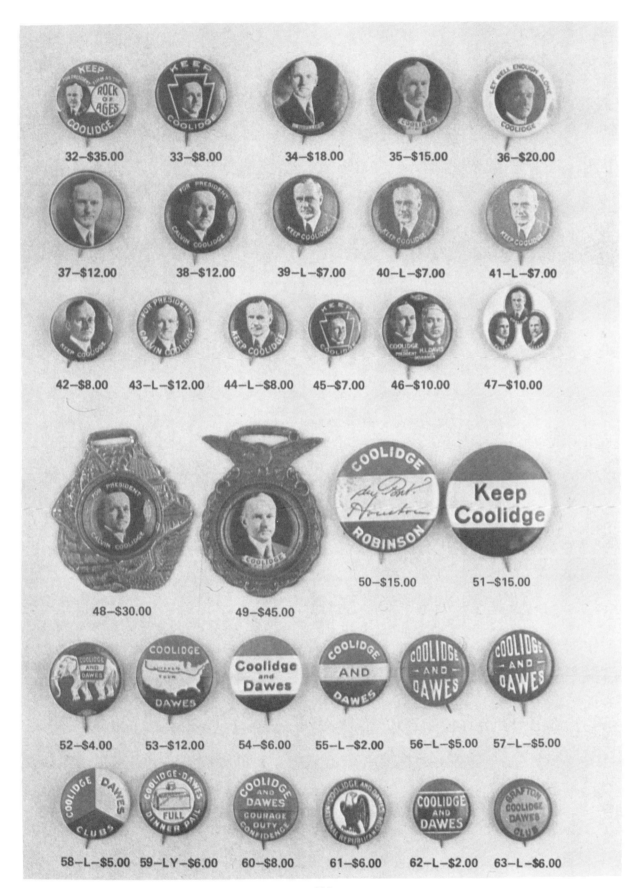

32—$35.00   33—$8.00   34—$18.00   35—$15.00   36—$20.00

37—$12.00   38—$12.00   39—L—$7.00   40—L—$7.00   41—L—$7.00

42—$8.00   43—L—$12.00   44—L—$8.00   45—$7.00   46—$10.00   47—$10.00

48—$30.00   49—$45.00   50—$15.00   51—$15.00

52—$4.00   53—$12.00   54—$6.00   55—L—$2.00   56—L—$5.00   57—L—$5.00

58—L—$5.00   59—LY—$6.00   60—$8.00   61—$6.00   62—L—$2.00   63—L—$6.00

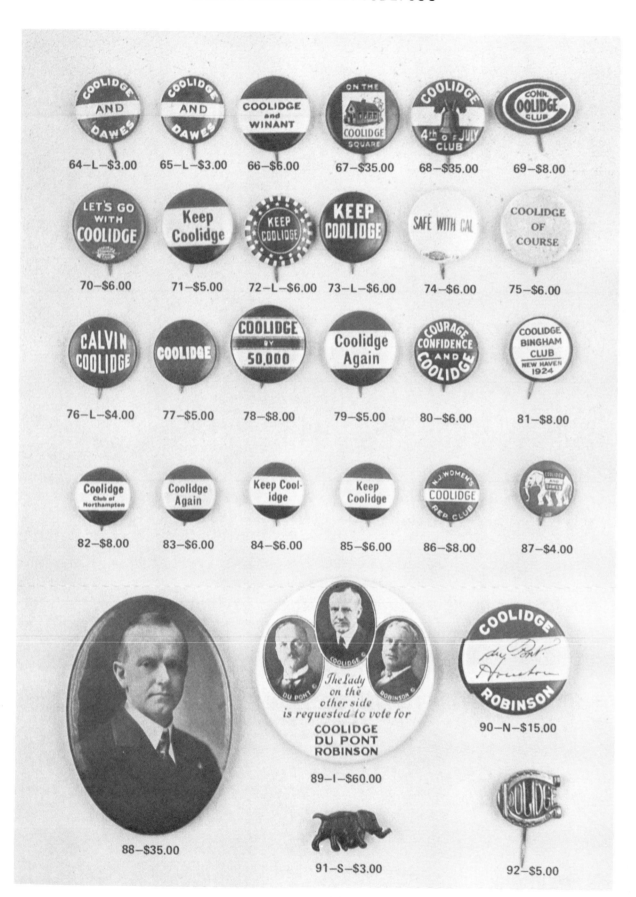

64—L—$3.00   65—L—$3.00   66—$6.00   67—$35.00   68—$35.00   69—$8.00

70—$6.00   71—$5.00   72—L—$6.00   73—L—$6.00   74—$6.00   75—$6.00

76—L—$4.00   77—$5.00   78—$8.00   79—$5.00   80—$6.00   81—$8.00

82—$8.00   83—$6.00   84—$6.00   85—$6.00   86—$8.00   87—$4.00

88—$35.00   89—I—$60.00   90—N—$15.00

91—S—$3.00   92—$5.00

JOHN W. DAVIS – DEMOCRAT

Campaign	1924
	LOST
Electoral Votes	136
Popular Votes	8,386,704
Running Mate	CHARLES W. BRYAN
Convention	NEW YORK CITY
Birth	CLARKSBURG, WEST VIRGINIA, APRIL 13, 1873
Death	MARCH 24, 1955

After seventeen days and one hundred and three ballots, John W. Davis became the 1924 Democratic nominee. The convention had turned into a hopeless deadlock split on the issue of the Ku Klux Klan. Anti-Klan delegates stood staunchly behind Alfred E. Smith of New York. The pro-Klan delegates backed William G. McAdoo, although he disavowed some of the Klan's principles. Smith's Catholicism made him particularly unaccepted to the pro-Klan forces. Davis, a former West Virginia congressman and leading Wall Street lawyer, became the compromise candidate. His running mate was Charles W. Bryan, Governor of Nebraska, whose main qualification consisted of being William Jennings Bryan's brother.

The Democrats tried to win the election with the issue of the Teapot Dome scandals and devised the slogan "Honest Days With Davis." Coolidge refused to become personally involved in the scandal question. The fact that he did launch a government investigation helped maintain the people's trust in the President. The result was three hundred and two electoral votes for Coolidge, one hundred thirty-six for Davis, and thirteen for Robert M. LaFollette running on the Progressive and Socialist Party tickets.

The Progressive Party aimed at a coalition of farmers and workers designed to "break the power of the private monopoly system over the economic and political life of the American people." LaFollette's running mate was Burton K. Wheeler. The Progressives received nearly five million votes, but even with this support Davis would have lost to Coolidge.

Overall, Davis buttons are even rarer than James Cox buttons. Even Davis name buttons are rare. Collectors must be sure that "Davis" name buttons apply to John W. Davis as there have been numerous candidates named "Davis" for local and state offices. Davis and Bryan jugates are second in value to the Cox and Roosevelt jugates and are extremely rare. The Democrats did have more money to spend in 1924 than 1920, but not much of it was used for the purchase of campaign items. There are about five buttons of particular interest since they make reference to the Teapot Dome oil scandals. Most of these picture a teapot as part of the graphics.

1—$300.00

2—R—$35.00

3—$100.00

4—$75.00

5—$95.00

6—$95.00

7—$75.00

8—$75.00

9—$70.00

10—$75.00

11—Z—$50.00

12—$65.00

13—$70.00

14—$40.00

15—L—$30.00

16—LY—$25.00

17—L—$25.00

18—L—$40.00

19—L—$40.00

20—$25.00

21—$30.00

22—$25.00

23—$25.00

24—$25.00

25—$25.00

26–$350.00

27–$125.00

28–$95.00

29–R–$25.00

30–$85.00

31–L–$35.00

32–$80.00

33–$60.00

34–L–$70.00

35–$45.00

36–L–$25.00

37–L–$20.00

JOHN W. DAVIS
HELP MAKE A GREAT
WEST VIRGINIAN
PRESIDENT

38–R–$5.00

39–L–$25.00

HERBERT C. HOOVER — REPUBLICAN

Campaigns	1928	1932
	WON	LOST
Electoral Votes	444	59
Popular Votes	21,437,277	15,760,684
Running Mates	CHARLES CURTIS	CHARLES CURTIS
Conventions	KANSAS CITY, MO.	CHICAGO
Birth	WEST BRANCH, IOWA, AUG. 10, 1874	
Death	OCT. 20, 1964	

When Calvin Coolidge announced his decision not to run for President in 1928, Herbert Hoover, Secretary of Commerce, became the leading contender. By convention time, Hoover's strength was sufficient to win the nomination on the first ballot. Senator Charles Curtis of Kansas became the running mate.

Prohibition, established by the Eighteenth Amendment, was a major issue and Hoover came out for its strict enforcement. His campaign was more active than that of Coolidge in 1924, but he avoided meeting his opponent Al Smith in public debate. He managed not to mention Smith's name once during the entire campaign. Hoover denounced the bigots who attacked Smith because he was Catholic. Americans, however, were swamped with vicious written propaganda that encouraged them to believe American policy would be dictated by the Pope if Smith were elected.

The election was another Republican landslide. At his inauguration Hoover said: "We have reached a higher degree of comfort and security that ever existed before in the history of the world." Seven months later the stock market crashed and shattered the dreams of thousands of Americans. Hoover continually issued reassurances that the worst was over. He refused to engage in public works projects and staunchly defended a balanced budget. In 1930, the Republican Congress passed a high tariff that outraged other countries and drastically reduced the market for American goods.

Hoover ran for re-election in 1932 and believed he had done everything in the government's power to pull the country out of the depression. He felt F.D.R. proposed "changes and so-called new deals which would destroy the very foundations of our American system." The people felt differently and Roosevelt won four hundred seventy-two electoral votes to Hoover's fifty-nine. Hoover left office a much abused man, but continued his public service in various positions into the 1950's. In 1964, he died at age ninety.

The Republican elephant was a frequently used symbol on Hoover items. A few name buttons are common, but most picture buttons sell for over ten dollars. A wider variety of jugates were used than in the few preceding elections. Most jugates are scarce and sell for fifty dollars or more.

1–$150.00   2–$150.00   3–Z–$125.00   4–$100.00

5–$100.00   6–L–$60.00   7–Z–$60.00   8–$40.00   9–$75.00

10–L–$50.00   11–$35.00

12–$45.00   13–$10.00

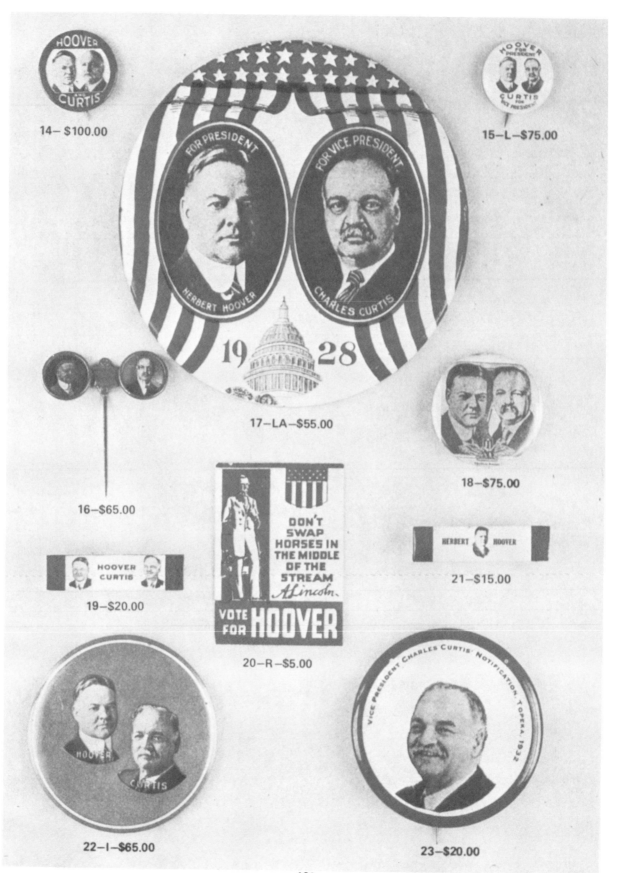

14— $100.00

15—L—$75.00

17—LA—$55.00

16—$65.00

18—$75.00

19—$20.00

DON'T SWAP HORSES IN THE MIDDLE OF THE STREAM A.Lincoln.

VOTE FOR HOOVER

21—$15.00

20—R—$5.00

22—I—$65.00

23—$20.00

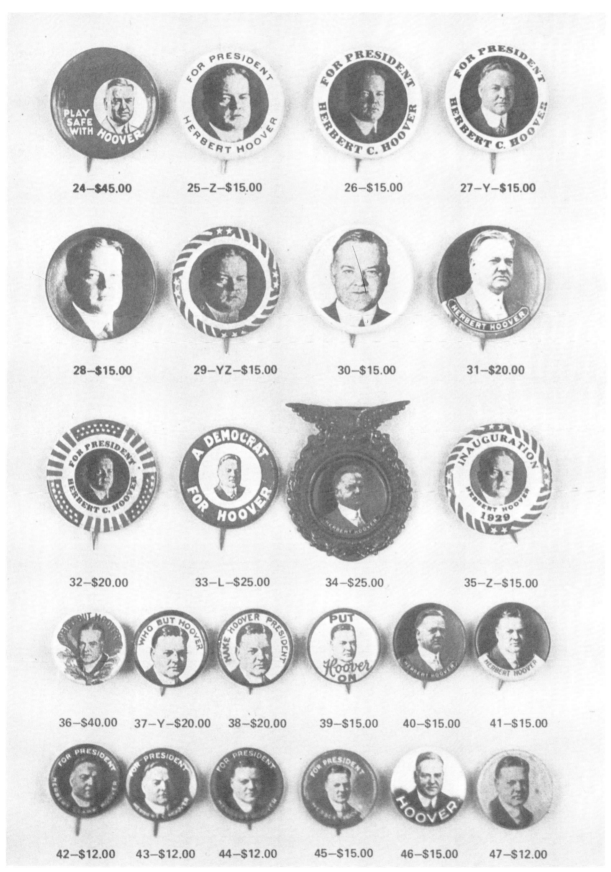

24—$45.00   25—Z—$15.00   26—$15.00   27—Y—$15.00

28—$15.00   29—YZ—$15.00   30—$15.00   31—$20.00

32—$20.00   33—L—$25.00   34—$25.00   35—Z—$15.00

36—$40.00   37—Y—$20.00   38—$20.00   39—$15.00   40—$15.00   41—$15.00

42—$12.00   43—$12.00   44—$12.00   45—$15.00   46—$15.00   47—$12.00

48—$12.00   49—$12.00   50—$15.00   51—$20.00   52—$15.00   53—$12.00

54—L—$15.00   55—L—$20.00   56—L—$20.00   57—L—$20.00   58—L—$18.00   59—L—$18.00

60—$20.00   61—$20.00   62—$20.00   63—LY—$18.00   64—L—$15.00   65—$14.00

66—L—$10.00   67—$3.00   68—L—$5.00   69—L—$5.00   70—L—$5.00

71—$20.00   72—$10.00   73—$8.00   74—N—$12.00

75—L—$5.00   76—L—$4.00   77—L—$3.00   78—L—$2.00   79—L—$4.00   80—L—$3.00

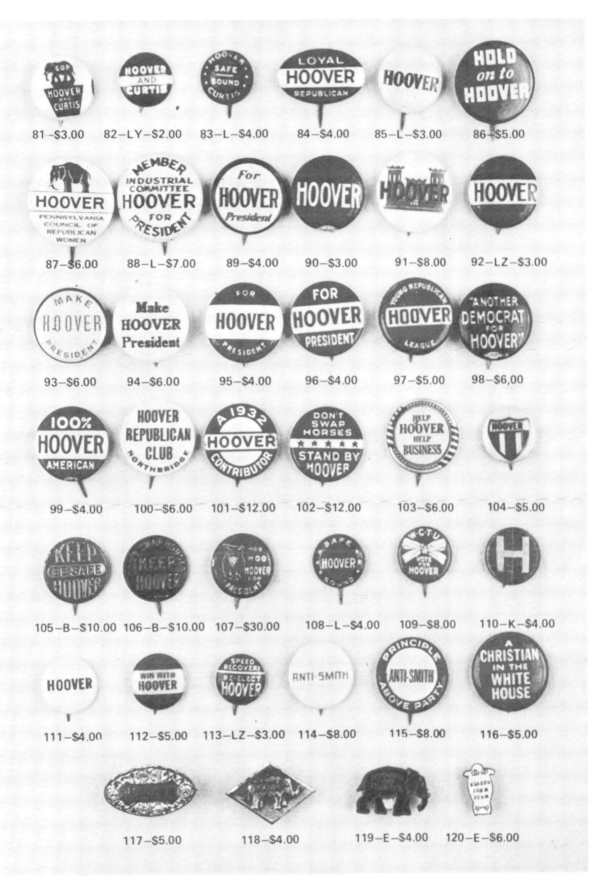

81 – $3.00   82 – LY – $2.00   83 – L – $4.00   84 – $4.00   85 – L – $3.00   86 – $5.00

87 – $6.00   88 – L – $7.00   89 – $4.00   90 – $3.00   91 – $8.00   92 – LZ – $3.00

93 – $6.00   94 – $6.00   95 – $4.00   96 – $4.00   97 – $5.00   98 – $6,00

99 – $4.00   100 – $6.00   101 – $12.00   102 – $12.00   103 – $6.00   104 – $5.00

105 – B – $10.00   106 – B – $10.00   107 – $30.00   108 – L – $4.00   109 – $8.00   110 – K – $4.00

111 – $4.00   112 – $5.00   113 – LZ – $3.00   114 – $8.00   115 – $8.00   116 – $5.00

117 – $5.00   118 – $4.00   119 – E – $4.00   120 – E – $6.00

122–LM–$12.00

121–A–$30.00

123–$25.00

124–$25.00

125–U–$15.00

126–$10.00

127–$5.00

128–$4.00

129–U–$4.00

130–K–$4.00

131–$4.00

132–L–$20.00

133–$25.00

134–$25.00

135–$25.00

136–$5.00

137–$15.00

138–$12.00

139–$35.00

140–$5.00

141–U–$5.00

142–U–$5.00

143–I–$25.00

144–R–$4.00

145–$35.00

146–R–$4.00

ALFRED E. SMITH — DEMOCRAT

Campaigns	1928
	LOST
Electoral Votes	87
Popular Votes	15,007,698
Running Mate	JOSEPH T. ROBINSON
Conventions	HOUSTON
Birth	NEW YORK, N.Y., DEC. 30, 1873
Death	OCT. 5, 1944

In September 1927, William McAdoo, champion of the rural South and West, announced he would not be a candidate for the Democratic nomination in 1928. This opened the way for Governor Alfred E. Smith of New York to win the nomination he had been seeking since 1920. Smith was the first Catholic nominated for President. He was also a big city politician and known to be opposed to strict enforcement of prohibition. His running mate, Senator Joseph T. Robinson of Arkansas, was a Protestant and prohibitionist who was added to the ticket for balance.

Smith constantly toured the country and attacked the Republicans, but his efforts were futile. The public expected "Coolidge prosperity" to continue with Hoover and voted accordingly. Smith failed to carry his home state of New York and won in only eight states. The result was four hundred forty-four electoral votes for Hoover to eighty-seven for Smith.

Smith was honest and progressive. The reason for his lost battles at earlier conventions and in 1928 was summed up by H.L. Mencken: "Those who fear the Pope outnumber those who are tired of the Anti-Saloon League."

In 1932, Smith was again a leading contender and might have won in spite of the bias against his religion had the Democrats nominated him. However, Smith lost the nomination to Franklin Delano Roosevelt, the man who had placed Smith's name in nomination three times in the past. Smith later became a bitter party maverick critical of Roosevelt and the New Deal.

Al Smith's brown derby hat became the most frequently used symbol on campaign items. There were metal pins in the hat shape and small celluloid replicas of the hat were often suspended from campaign buttons. Enamel donkeys wearing brown derbies were also issued. The Democratic campaign chest was further improved since 1920 and 1924 with a consequent increase in the number of campaign items. Still there are only several common picture and name buttons, and jugates are scarce and worth over fifty dollars each.

ALFRED E. SMITH 1928 CODE: SMI

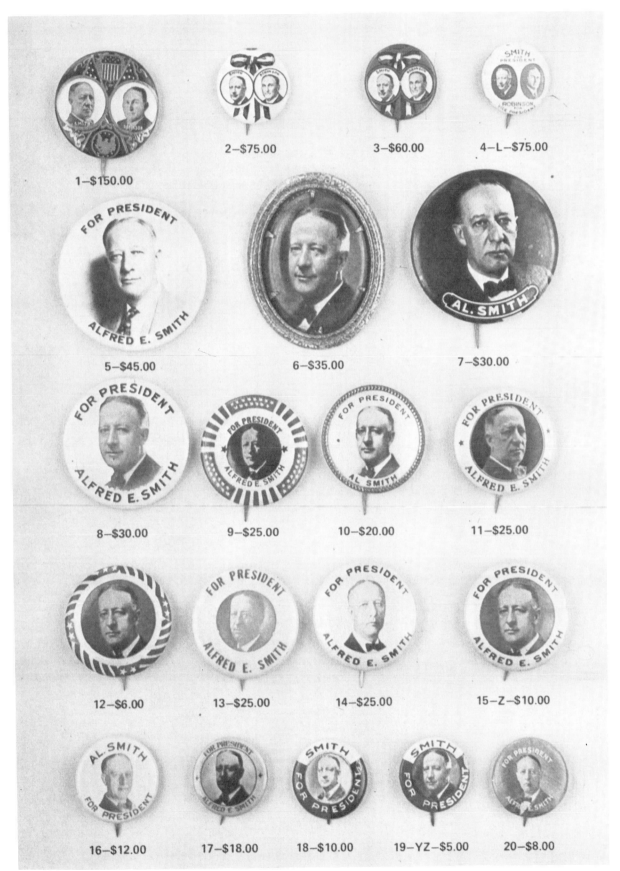

1—$150.00

2—$75.00

3—$60.00

4—L—$75.00

5—$45.00

6—$35.00

7—$30.00

8—$30.00

9—$25.00

10—$20.00

11—$25.00

12—$6.00

13—$25.00

14—$25.00

15—Z—$10.00

16—$12.00

17—$18.00

18—$10.00

19—YZ—$5.00

20—$8.00

21—$75.00

22—L—$75.00

24—LA—$150.00

23—$40.00

25—$18.00

26—$20.00

27—A—$50.00

28—$15.00

29—$12.00 30—$15.00 31—Y—$12.00 32—$18.00 33—$18.00 34—$15.00

35—LY $5.00 36—L—$5.00 37—L—$25.00 38—$15.00 39—$15.00

40—$15.00 41—$20.00 42—$20.00 43—$20.00 44—$15.00 45—L—$6.00

46—$15.00 47—$20.00 48—$15.00 49—B—$20.00 50—B—$20.00

51—L—$30.00 52—$10.00 53—$5.00 54—L—$6.00 55—L—$6.00 56—L—$15.00

57—L—$10.00 58—$25.00 59—$10.00 60—L—$15.00 61—$8.00 62—$10.00

ALFRED E. SMITH 1928 CODE: SMI

63 – $8.00   64 – $8.00   65 – E – $12.00   66 – $12.00   67 – L – $12.00   68 – S – $8.00

69 – $25.00   70 – $25.00   71 – $25.00   72 – $15.00

73 – U – $15.00   74 – U – $10.00   75 – $30.00   76 – $5.00   77 – $5.00

78 – $6.00   79 – E – $6.00   80 – E – $6.00   81 – E – $6.00   82 – E – $8.00

83 – $12.00   84 – $18.00   85 – $5.00   86 – $22.00   87 – $20.00   88 – $4.00

130

89–L–$20.00

90–$25.00

91–$15.00

92–L–$20.00

93–I–$40.00

94–L–$20.00

95–$25.00

96–$10.00

97–$20.00

98–$8.00

99–$10.00

100–L–$25.00

101–L–$10.00

102–E–$6.00

103–A–$30.00

104–$25.00

FRANKLIN DELANO ROOSEVELT — DEMOCRAT

Campaigns	1932	1936	1940	1944
	WON	WON	WON	WON
Electoral Votes	472	523	449	432
Popular Votes	22,829,501	27,757,333	27,313,041	25,612,610
Running Mates	JOHN N. GARNER	JOHN N. GARNER	HENRY A. WALLACE	HARRY S. TRUMAN
Conventions	CHICAGO	PHILADELPHIA	CHICAGO	CHICAGO
Birth	HYDE PARK, N.Y., JAN. 30, 1882			
Death	APRIL 12, 1945			

Franklin D. Roosevelt spent twelve years and forty days in the Presidency. During that time, his actions precipitated both intense loyalty and opposition. F.D.R.'s enemies saw him as "that Red in the White House," while his admirers felt he acted on behalf of the poor, the minorities and the working class.

After Groton, Harvard, and Columbia University Law School, F.D.R.'s political career began in 1910 when he ran for the New York State Senate. He won by a slim margin and was re-elected in 1912. F.D.R. gave his support to Woodrow Wilson at the 1912 convention and this led to his appointment as Assistant Secretary of the Navy. He supported Alfred E. Smith at the 1920 convention, but the delegates chose James M. Cox, who in turn chose F.D.R. as his running mate. The election was lost, and F.D.R. joined a law firm until suddenly struck by infantile paralysis. After much pain, he slowly improved which gave him the hope needed to mentally overcome his handicap. Later he said, "If you have spent two years in bed trying to wiggle your big toe, everything else seems easy."

F.D.R. made a brief return to national politics in 1924 as head of Alfred E. Smith's campaign in New York State. At Madison Square Garden, F.D.R. was able to take ten steps alone to reach the rostrum for his convention address. He received a tremendous ovation for his courage and triumph over his disease.

Smith finally won the Democratic nomination in 1928 and he wanted F.D.R. to run for Governor of New York. F.D.R. refused, but after the convention nominated him by acclamation he accepted. While Republicans complained of his "unfortunate" condition, F.D.R. traversed the state with great enthusiasm. His victory by twenty-five thousand votes was slim but allowed him to carry on Smith's progressive programs with additions of his own. His re-election in 1930 was a great victory. He won by some seven hundred thousand votes, making him the front runner for the 1932 presidential nomination.

F.D.R.'s four presidential victories produced a large number of campaign items. Most jugates are scarce and sell for over thirty dollars, but there are several very common designs that sell for less. Single picture buttons were frequently issued for more than one campaign so these are difficult to date accurately. Picture buttons are generally in the two to five dollar range. The 1¼" slogan button was a primary feature of the 1940 campaign against Willkie. There are even more Willkie slogan buttons that protest F.D.R.'s unprecedented try for a third term.

FRANKLIN D. ROOSEVELT 1932, 1936, 1940, 1944 CODE: FDR

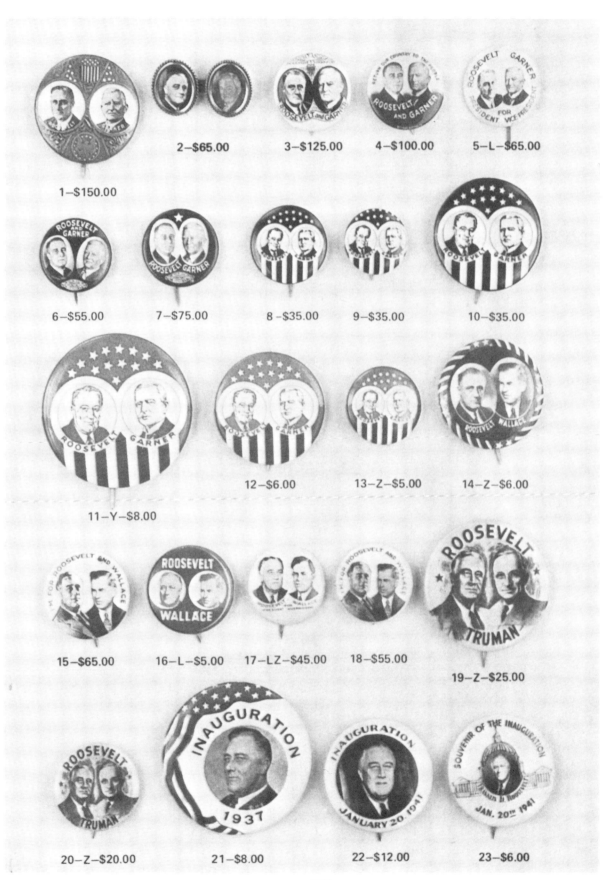

1—$150.00

2—$65.00

3—$125.00

4—$100.00

5—L—$65.00

6—$55.00

7—$75.00

8—$35.00

9—$35.00

10—$35.00

11—Y—$8.00

12—$6.00

13—Z—$5.00

14—Z—$6.00

15—$65.00

16—L—$5.00

17—LZ—$45.00

18—$55.00

19—Z—$25.00

20—Z—$20.00

21—$8.00

22—$12.00

23—$6.00

24—$20.00

25—LM—$6.00

26—$25.00

27—L—$25.00

28—$15.00

29—$15.00

FRANKLIN D. ROOSEVELT 1932, 1936, 1940, 1944 CODE: FDR

30–$18.00

31–$18.00

32–$8.00

33–$8.00

34–$8.00

35–$10.00

36–$14.00

37–$10.00

38–$10.00

39–$8.00

40–$6.00

41–$6.00

42–$10.00

43–$10.00

44–$12.00

45–$10.00

46–$5.00

47–$5.00

48–L–$5.00

49–$5.00

50—$15.00   51—$8.00   52—$8.00   53—$8.00

54—$10.00   55—$4.00   56—Z—$8.00   57—$10.00

58—$6.00   59—$8.00   60—$6.00   61—$10.00

62—$3.00   63—$2.00   64—Y- $3.00   65—$6.00

66—L—$3.00   67—L—$1.00   68—L—$4.00   69—L—$4.00

70—$4.00   71—Y—$3.00   72—Z—$3.00   73—$2.00

74—Z—$2.00   75—$4.00   76—$5.00   77—$5.00

78—$3.00   79—$4.00   80—L—$3.00   81—$2.00

82—L—$2.00   83—$1.00   84—$4.00   85—$3.00   86—$4.00

87—L—$4.00   88—L—$5.00   89—L—$3.00   90—L—$4.00   91—L—$5.00   92—L—$3.00   93—$4.00

FRANKLIN D. ROOSEVELT 1932, 1936, 1940, 1944 CODE: FDR

94—$10.00   95—$8.00   96—$6.00   97—$8.00   98—$10.00

99—$5.00   100—$5.00   101—$5.00   102—$5.00   103—$4.00   104—$4.00

105—$2.00   106—$2.00   107—$3.00   108—$3.00   109—$3.00   110—$6.00

111—$4.00   112—$4.00   113—$4.00   114—$4.00   115—$4.00   116—$4.00

117—$6.00   118—$4.00   119—$5.00   120—L—$5.00   121—$5.00   122—L—$4.00

123—L—$2.00   124—L—$6.00   125—L—$1.00   126—L—$3.00   127—L—$8.00   128—L—$8.00

129—Z—$2.00   130—$2.00   131—$4.00   132—L—$2.00   133—L—$1.00   134—L—$1.00

135—$4.00   136—$3.00   137—$4.00   138—$4.00   139—$8.00

140—L—$6.00   141—L—$5.00   142—L—$4.00   143—L—$1.00   144—L—$1.00

145—L—$4.00   146—L—$5.00   147—L—$3.00   148—L—$3.00   149—L—$5.00

150—L—$4.00   151—L—$2.00   152—L—$2.00   153—L—$3.00   154—L—$3.00

155—$12.00

157—$18.00

156—$15.00

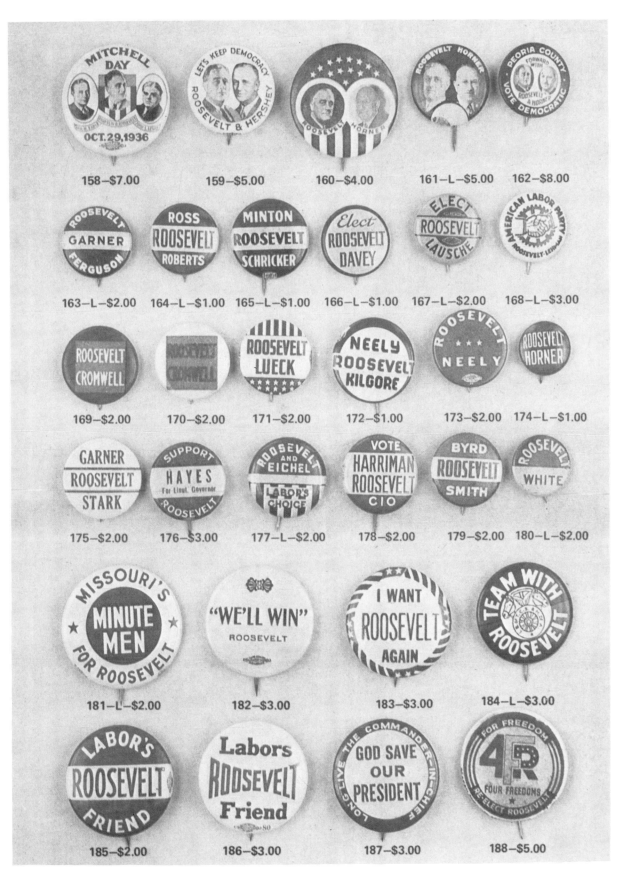

158—$7.00   159—$5.00   160—$4.00   161—L—$5.00   162—$8.00

163—L—$2.00 164—L—$1.00 165—L—$1.00 166—L—$1.00 167—L—$2.00 168—L—$3.00

169—$2.00   170—$2.00   171—$2.00   172—$1.00   173—$2.00   174—L—$1.00

175—$2.00   176—$3.00   177—L—$2.00   178—$2.00   179—$2.00   180—L—$2.00

181—L—$2.00   182—$3.00   183—$3.00   184—L—$3.00

185—$2.00   186—$3.00   187—$3.00   188—$5.00

Confucius Say........
ONE TIME - GOOD
TWO TIME - GOOD
THREE TIME -
DAMN GOOD

189—$2.00

A THIRD TERM
is BETTER
than a THIRD
RATER

190—$1.00

WE
DON'T
THROW
ROTTEN
EGGS

191—$1.00

IF
WILLKIE'S
IN
WHITEHOUSE
IT'S U.S. IN
POORHOUSE

192—$1.00

FRIENDLY
DEPENDABLE
RESOURCEFUL

193—$1.00

I'LL
BET MY
B. V. D.
ON
F.D.R.

194—$1.00

WILLKIE
FOR THE
MILLIONAIRES
ROOSEVELT
FOR THE
MILLIONS

195—$2.00

WATCH
WILLKIE
WILT

196—$1.00

TWO
GOOD TIMES
DESERVE
ANOTHER

197—$1.00

REPEAT WITH
ROOSEVELT
OR REPENT
WITH WILLKIE

198—$1.00

KEEP
ROOSEVELT
IN
WHITEHOUSE
WILLKIE
IN
POWERHOUSE

199—$1.00

WILLKIE
FOR PRESIDENT
OF
COMMONWEALTH
AND
SOUTHERN

200—$1.00

WIN
WHAT ?
WITH
WILLKIE

201—$1.00

F. RANKLIN
D. ESERVES
R. EELECTION

202—$1.00

A
PAUPER
FOR
ROOSEVELT

203—Z—$1.00

FDR
CARRY ON

204—$1.00

WILLKIE?
NO! NO!
1000 TIMES NO!

205—$1.00

WE
MILLIONAIRES
WANT
WILLKIE

206—$1.00

AMERICA
WANTS
ROOSEVELT

207—$2.00

I Gotta Go
AND VOTE FOR
FDR

208—$1.00

142

209–L–$3.00   210–L $3.00   211–L–$4.00   212–BDN–$3.00   213–DN $3.00   214–$3.00

215–L–$2.00   216–L–$2.00   217–L–$4.00   218–$3.00

219–LY–$8.00   220–L–$8.00   221–L–$4.00   222–L–$4.00   223–L–$3.00

224–$4.00   225–L–$3.00   226–L–$3.00   227–L–$3.00   228–L–$4.00   229–$4.00

230–$3.00   231–$2.00   232–$3.00   233–$2.00   234–$2.00   235–$6.00

236–$2.00   237–$2.00   238–$2.00   239–B–$2.00   240–L–$4.00   241–L–$3.00

242–$3.00   243–$4.00   244–$5.00   245–$3.00   246–$3.00

247 –$3.00 248 –$4.00 249 –$3.00 250–$2.00 251–$2.00 252–$3.00

253–$1.00 254–$3.00 255–$1.00 256 –$2.00 257–$1.00 258 –$1.00

259–$1.00 260–$2.00 261–$2.00 262–$4.00 263–$3.00 264–L–$3.00

265–L–$1.00 266–LY–$1.00 267–L–$2.00 268–L–$1.00 269–$2.00 270–L–$3.00

271–L–$1.00 272–L–$1.00 273–L–$2.00 274–L–$3.00 275–L–$3.00

276–$3.00 277–L–$2.00 278–L–$2.00 279–L–$3.00 280–$3.00

281–L–$3.00 282–L–$2.00 283–L–$2.00 284–L–$3.00 285–$3.00

FRANKLIN D. ROOSEVELT 1932, 1936, 1940, 1944 CODE: FDR

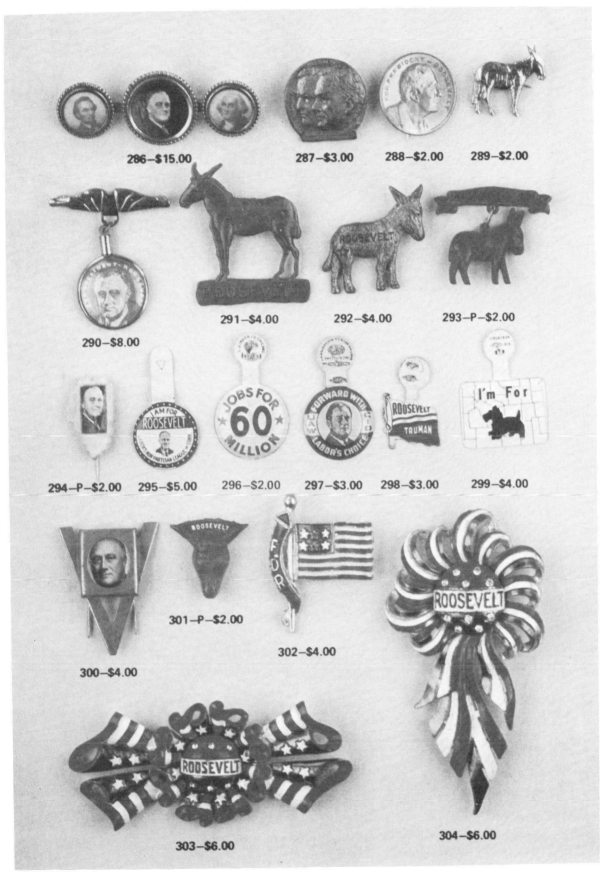

286—$15.00   287—$3.00   288—$2.00   289—$2.00

290—$8.00   291—$4.00   292—$4.00   293—P—$2.00

294—P—$2.00   295—$5.00   296—$2.00   297—$3.00   298—$3.00   299—$4.00

300—$4.00   301—P—$2.00

302—$4.00

303—$6.00   304—$6.00

305—$100.00   306—$15.00   307—$6.00

308—$8.00

309—$25.00   310—$10.00   311—$4.00   312—$5.00   313—$5.00

314—L—$8.00   315—$12.00   316—$15.00   317—$5.00   318—$10.00   319—$8.00

320—P—$3.00   321—L—$3.00

322—$3.00   323—C—$12.00   324—L—$3.00

ALFRED LANDON – REPUBLICAN

Campaign	1936
	LOST
Electoral Votes	8
Popular Votes	16,684,231
Running Mate	FRANK KNOX
Convention	CLEVELAND
Birth	WEST MIDDLESEX, PA., SEPT. 9, 1887

When the Republicans met in 1936 the country was by no means out of the depression, but it was recovering. Alfred Landon, Governor of Kansas, was chosen on the first ballot to try to defeat F.D.R. at the height of his popularity. Frank Knox, publisher of the Chicago *Daily News*, was Landon's running mate.

The Republican platform made many accusations: the President had usurped the powers of Congress, the authority of the Supreme Court had been "flaunted" and the "rights and liberties of American citizens" had been violated. To counter these violations, the Republicans pledged to "maintain the American system of constitutional and local self-government," to preserve free enterprise, and to provide "encouragement instead of hindrance to legitimate business."

Landon's symbol was the sunflower, the state flower of Kansas, and his main slogan was "Life, Liberty and Landon." The campaign began with Landon characterized as the "silent Coolidge from Kansas," but Republican advisors convinced Landon to be more agressive. He then charged F.D.R. with "willful waste" of taxpayer's money and the "strangling of free enterprise."

The President was cheered by crowds wherever he spoke, but most newspapers severely criticized him. The people's enthusiasm was reflected on election day when Landon won only Maine and Vermont for eight electoral votes. F.D.R.'s victory also gave the Democrats a wide margin of control in the House and Senate.

The sunflower motif appears on many Landon items either as part of the button design or as a piece of yellow felt that was slipped on the pinback. However, few campaign items can compare to the nineteen-petal gold and yellow diamond sunflower that a rich Republican could buy from Tiffany's for eight hundred fifteen dollars. Landon jugates with line drawing pictures are rather common, but those with photographic pictures are rare.

Two of the most popular Landon buttons make a play on the candidate's name. One shows a plane flying over the Capitol with the slogan "Land On Washington." The other button shows the "GOP" elephant landing on top of and collapsing the Democratic donkey with the slogan "Landon On the New Deal." Popular anti-Landon slogans were "We Can't Eat Sunflowers" and "Sunflowers Die In November."

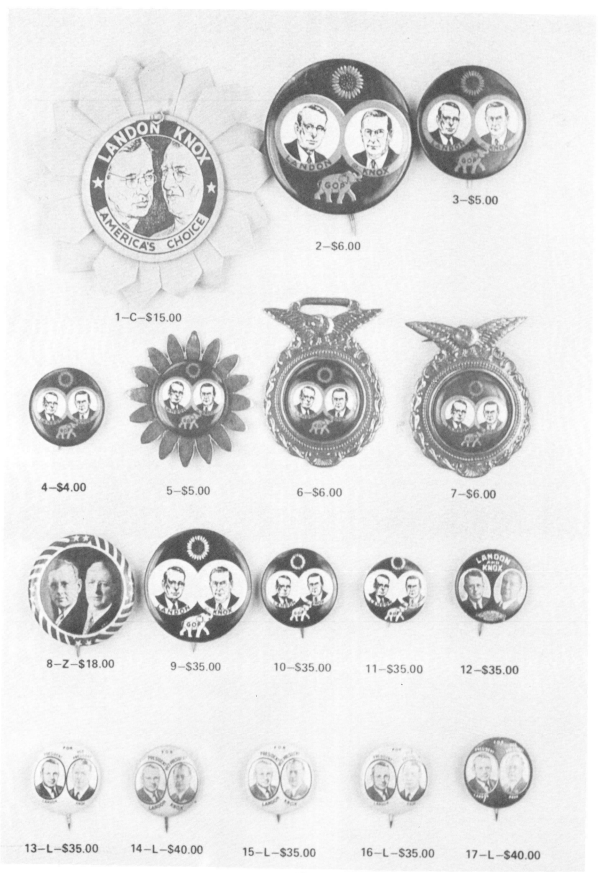

1—C—$15.00

2—$6.00

3—$5.00

4—$4.00

5—$5.00

6—$6.00

7—$6.00

8—Z—$18.00

9—$35.00

10—$35.00

11—$35.00

12—$35.00

13—L—$35.00

14—L—$40.00

15—L—$35.00

16—L—$35.00

17—L—$40.00

18—$25.00

19—$10.00

20—$10.00

21—Y—$4.00

22—$5.00

23—$4.00

24—$40.00

25—$15.00

26—L—$20.00

27—$10.00

28—Y—$6.00

29—$6.00

30—$5.00

31—$10.00

32—$25.00   33—$35.00   34—$10.00   35—$8.00   36—$10.00

37—$12.00   38—$12.00   39—$20.00   40—$30.00   41—$10.00   42—$35.00

43—$10.00   44—B—$10.00   45—B—$10.00   46—Z—$4.00   47—Y—$5.00   48—$12.00

49—$10.00   50—$3.00   51—$3.00   52—$5.00

53—$5.00   54—$5.00   55—$7.00   56—$4.00   57—$3.00

58—$12.00   59—$5.00   60—$6.00   61—N—$12.00

62—$5.00   63—$5.00   64—$7.00   65—$10.00

66—$5.00   67—Y—$4.00   68—$4.00   69—$6.00

70—$6.00   71—$8.00   72—$8.00   73—$8.00   74—$4.00   75—$4.00

76—$6.00   77—Z—$4.00   78—$6.00   79—$6.00   80—$5.00   81—$5.00

82—$3.00   83—$3.00   84—Y—$1.00   85—L—$4.00   86—L—$2.00   87—B—$4.00

88—L—$1.00   89—L—$1.00   90—L—$1.00   91—L—$1.00   92—L—$2.00   93—$3.00

ALFRED M. LANDON 1936 CODE: LAN

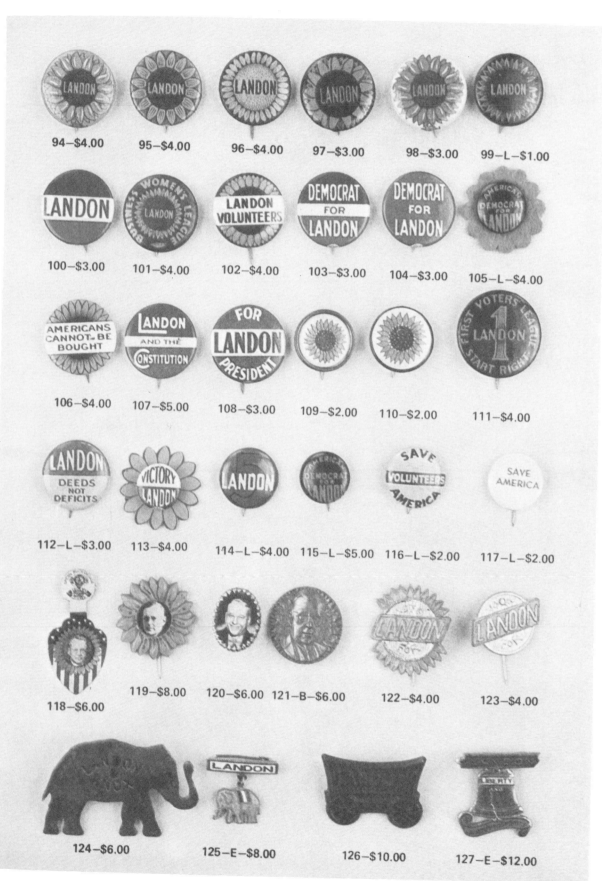

94—$4.00   95—$4.00   96—$4.00   97—$3.00   98—$3.00   99—L—$1.00

100—$3.00   101—$4.00   102—$4.00   103—$3.00   104—$3.00   105—L—$4.00

106—$4.00   107—$5.00   108—$3.00   109—$2.00   110—$2.00   111—$4.00

112—L—$3.00   113—$4.00   114—L—$4.00   115—L—$5.00   116—L—$2.00   117—L—$2.00

118—$6.00   119—$8.00   120—$6.00   121—B—$6.00   122—$4.00   123—$4.00

124—$6.00   125—E—$8.00   126—$10.00   127—E—$12.00

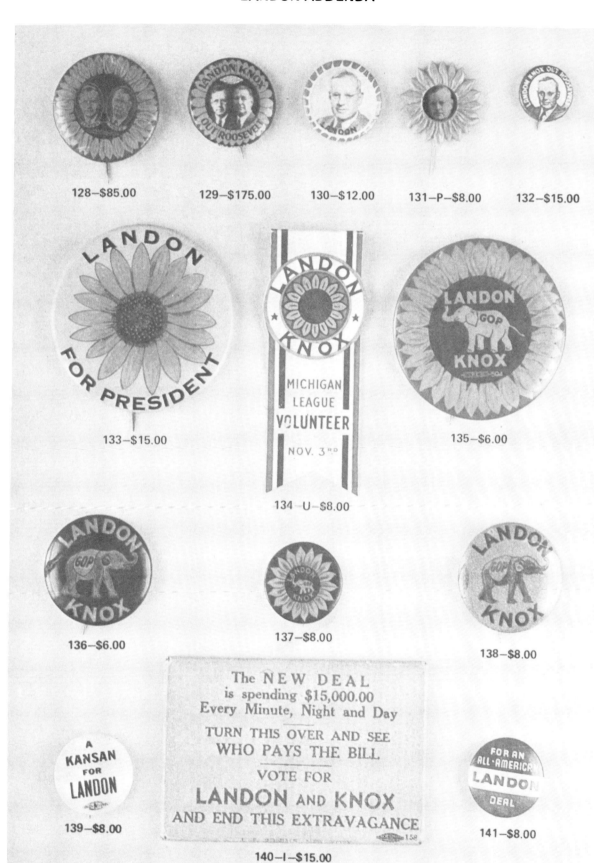

128—$85.00

129—$175.00

130—$12.00

131—P—$8.00

132—$15.00

133—$15.00

134—U—$8.00

135—$6.00

136—$6.00

137—$8.00

138—$8.00

139—$8.00

140—I—$15.00

141—$8.00

WENDELL L. WILLKIE – REPUBLICAN

Campaign	1940
	LOST
Electoral Votes	82
Popular Votes	22,348,480
Running Mate	CHARLES L. McNARY
Convention	PHILADELPHIA
Birth	ELWOOD, IND., FEB. 18, 1892
Death	OCT. 8, 1944

As the 1940 convention approached, Republicans were optimistic because of gains made in the 1938 mid-term elections. Leading candidates for the nomination included Thomas Dewey of New York and Robert Taft of Ohio. Wendell L. Willkie, President of the Commonwealth and Southern Utilities Company, was also mentioned. This was due to the national attention he received in a battle with the government over private versus public control of utilities.

A few short months before the convention, "Willkie for President" and "Win with Willkie" clubs were formed all over the country. The money came largely from publishers and corporation businessmen who financed an effective publicity campaign, and the necessary enthusiasm came from people tired of politicians tied to the party line.

The Willkie campaign gradually gained influential supporters and peaked just when the balloting began. Dewey's lead lasted only through the first ballot, and then Taft and Willkie began to gain. On the third ballot, Willkie overtook Taft and on the fourth ballot he took the lead. As voting proceeded, the galleries were packed with people chanting "we want Willkie." On the sixth ballot Michigan and Pennsylvania switched their votes and gave Willkie the nomination. Charles L. McNary, minority leader of the Senate, was added to the ticket to rally isolationists and conservatives.

Willkie agreed with much of F.D.R.'s program, so the main issue became the President's decision to run for a third term. Willkie charged that F.D.R. thought himself "indispensable" and desired only to perpetuate "one-man rule." F.D.R. remained silent during the early stages of the campaign and devoted himself to running the nation. At the end of the campaign, Willkie's approach changed and he told audiences that a vote for Roosevelt would surely involve America in a foreign war. F.D.R. then made a series of speeches in defense of his administration. In the end, Americans decided to keep F.D.R. at the helm as war in Europe grew more threatening.

It is estimated that thirty-three million Willkie buttons were issued and twenty-one million for F.D.R. Most of these took the form of 1¼" slogan buttons and name buttons. Willkie buttons most frequently express opposition to F.D.R.'s third term. Compared to the slogan buttons, very few picture buttons and even fewer jugates were issued.

1–L–$35.00

2–$30.00

3–L–$30.00

4–L–$35.00

5–$8.00

6–$5.00

7–$5.00

8–$10.00

9–$5.00

10–N–$4.00

11–$3.00

WENDELL L. WILLKIE 1940 CODE: WIL

12—$8.00

13—$6.00

14—L—$5.00

15—$6.00

16—$6.00

17—$2.00

18—$2.00

19—$2.00

20—$4.00

21—$3.00

22—$2.00

23—$4.00

24—$4.00

25—$3.00

26—Y—$3.00

27—NY $4.00

28—$6.00

29—$3.00

30—$3.00

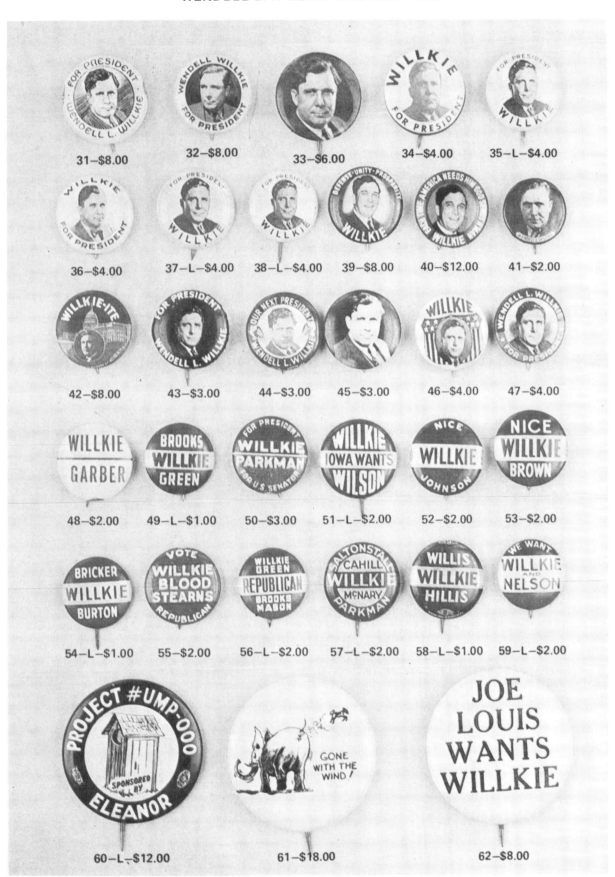

31—$8.00   32—$8.00   33—$6.00   34—$4.00   35—L—$4.00

36—$4.00   37—L—$4.00   38—L—$4.00   39—$8.00   40—$12.00   41—$2.00

42—$8.00   43—$3.00   44—$3.00   45—$3.00   46—$4.00   47—$4.00

48—$2.00   49—L—$1.00   50—$3.00   51—L—$2.00   52—$2.00   53—$2.00

54—L—$1.00   55—$2.00   56—L—$2.00   57—L—$2.00   58—L—$1.00   59—L—$2.00

60—L—$12.00   61—$18.00   62—$8.00

WENDELL L. WILLKIE 1940 CODE: WIL

UP-ON AMERICA WIN WITH WILLKIE
63—$6.00

ASSOCIATED WILLKIE CLUBS WILLKIE WORKERS OF PENNA.
64—$3.00

WILLKIE-McNARY CAMPAIGN CONTRIBUTOR "WILLKIE IS OUR MAN!" 423 TENTH WARD · ST. PAUL
65—$5.00

I'M AGAINST THE 3rd TERM WASHINGTON WOULDN'T GRANT COULDN'T ROOSEVELT SHOULDN'T
66—$3.00

JOE LOUIS FOR WILLKIE
67—$15.00

JOE AND I WANT WILLKIE
68—$15.00

8 YEARS IS PLENTY
69—$6.00

DOWN AND OUT
70—$2.00

THE LAST ACT
71—$2.00

I'LL BET MY ON WILLKIE
72—$2.00

WILLKIE McNARY
73—$1.00

NEW DEAL WASTE BASKET
74—$2.00

I'M BEHIND THE EIGHT BALL 8
75—$6.00

YOU LOSE FRANKLIN
76—$1.00

AWAY WITH NEW DEAL VOTE WILLKIE FOR PROSPERITY AND IT'S INEFFICIENCY
77—$4.00

WILL HE WILL!
78—$3.00

I'M AGAINST THE THIRD TERM WASHINGTON WOULDN'T GRANT COULDN'T ROOSEVELT SHOULDN'T
79—L—$2.00

MY SHOULDER TO THE WHEEL FOR WILLKIE
80—L—$5.00

SQUARE WILLKIE DEAL
81—L—$3.00

158

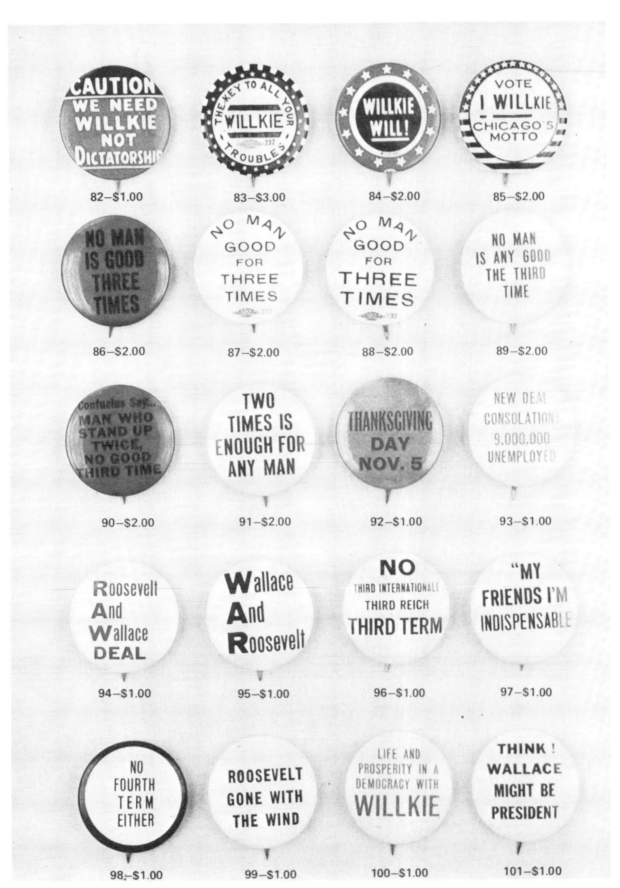

82—$1.00   83—$3.00   84—$2.00   85—$2.00

86—$2.00   87—$2.00   88—$2.00   89—$2.00

90—$2.00   91—$2.00   92—$1.00   93—$1.00

94—$1.00   95—$1.00   96—$1.00   97—$1.00

98—$1.00   99—$1.00   100—$1.00   101—$1.00

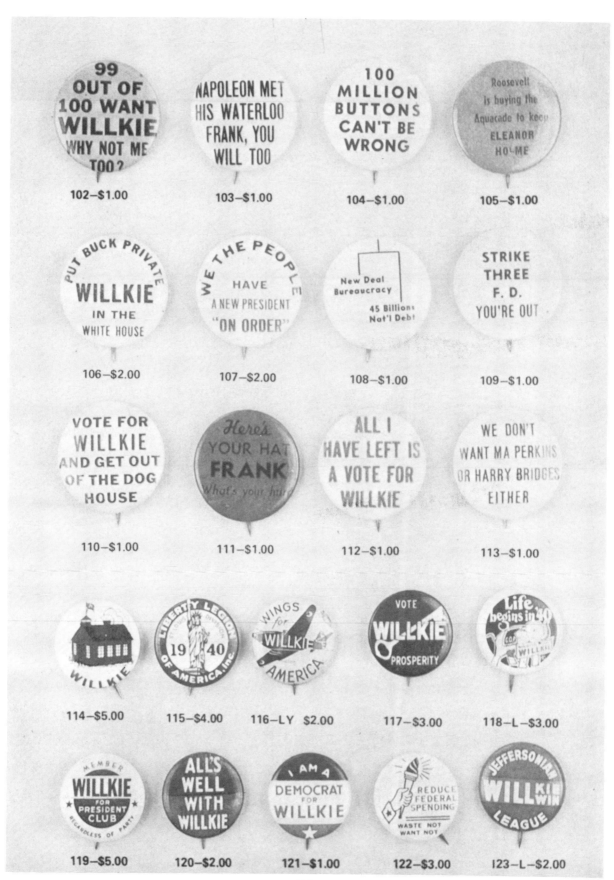

99 OUT OF 100 WANT WILLKIE WHY NOT ME TOO?

102–$1.00

NAPOLEON MET HIS WATERLOO FRANK, YOU WILL TOO

103–$1.00

100 MILLION BUTTONS CAN'T BE WRONG

104–$1.00

Roosevelt is buying the Aquacade to keep ELEANOR HOLME

105–$1.00

PUT BUCK PRIVATE WILLKIE IN THE WHITE HOUSE

106–$2.00

WE THE PEOPLE HAVE A NEW PRESIDENT "ON ORDER"

107–$2.00

New Deal Bureaucracy 45 Billions Nat'l Debt

108–$1.00

STRIKE THREE F. D. YOU'RE OUT

109–$1.00

VOTE FOR WILLKIE AND GET OUT OF THE DOG HOUSE

110–$1.00

Here's YOUR HAT FRANK What's your hurry

111–$1.00

ALL I HAVE LEFT IS A VOTE FOR WILLKIE

112–$1.00

WE DON'T WANT MA PERKINS OR HARRY BRIDGES EITHER

113–$1.00

WILLKIE

114–$5.00

LIBERTY LEGION OF AMERICA INC 19 40

115–$4.00

WINGS for WILLKIE AMERICA

116–LY $2.00

VOTE WILLKIE PROSPERITY

117–$3.00

Life begins in 40 WILLKIE

118–L–$3.00

MEMBER WILLKIE FOR PRESIDENT CLUB REGARDLESS OF PARTY

119–$5.00

ALL'S WELL WITH WILLKIE

120–$2.00

I AM A DEMOCRAT FOR WILLKIE

121–$1.00

REDUCE FEDERAL SPENDING WASTE NOT WANT NOT

122–$3.00

JEFFERSONIAN WILLKIE LEAGUE

123–L–$2.00

124—$4.00   125—$2.00   126—$2.00   127—$2.00   128—$5.00

129—$2.00   130—$2.00   131—L—$2.00   132—$2.00   133—L—$2.00   134—$1.00

135—L—$2.00   136—L—$2.00   137—$2.00   138—L—$2.00   139—$3.00   140—$3.00

141—$3.00   142—$2.00   143—$1.00   144—L—$1.00   145—$4.00   146—$3.00

147—L—$1.00   148—L—$1.00   149—L—$1.00   150—L—$1.00   151—L—$1.00   152—$2.00

153—$1.00   154—$2.00   155—$2.00   156—LY—$1.00   157—L—$3.00   158—$2.00

159—$4.00   160—$3.00   161—L—$2.00   162—L—$1.00   163—L—$1.00   164—$2.00

WENDELL L. WILLKIE 1940 CODE: WIL

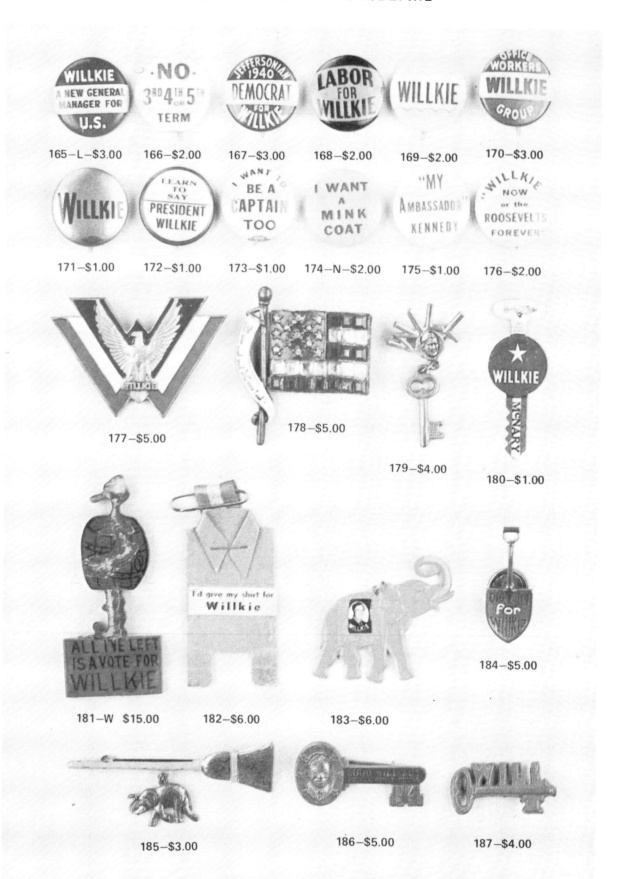

165-L—$3.00   166—$2.00   167—$3.00   168—$2.00   169—$2.00   170—$3.00

171—$1.00   172—$1.00   173—$1.00   174-N—$2.00   175—$1.00   176—$2.00

177—$5.00

178—$5.00

179—$4.00

180—$1.00

181-W $15.00   182—$6.00

183—$6.00

184—$5.00

185—$3.00

186—$5.00

187—$4.00

188—$5.00

189—WK—$2.00

190—P—$3.00

191—P—$3.00

192—P—$2.00

193—$2.00

194—$2.00

195—$2.00

196—E—$4.00

197—S—$3.00

198—$4.00

199—$5.00

200—E—$5.00

201—L—$8.00

I'm for WILLKIE
JOE LOUIS

202—$15.00

WILLKIE FOR PRESIDENT
W C R P O

205—$6.00

I Want WILLKIE

203—$4.00

204—$5.00

LET WILLKIE UNLOCK OPPORTUNITY

206—$6.00

JOE and ME FOR WILLKIE

207—$2.00

"ON OUR WAY"
UNITED STATES
MAINE
CALIFORNIA

208—$10.00

TENNESSEE WANTS WILLKIE AND McNARY 1940

209—$4.00

We Want WILLKIE McNARY

210—R—$1.00

211—R—$1.00

WILLKIE

212—R—$1.00

THINK
Hitler Nominated Hitler
Mussolini Nominated Mussolini
Stalin Nominated Stalin
Roosevelt Nominated Roosevelt
DO YOU WANT A DICTATOR?

213—C—$2.00

THOMAS E. DEWEY – REPUBLICAN

Campaigns	1944	1948
	LOST	LOST
Electoral Votes	99	189
Popular Votes	22,017,617	21,991,291
Running Mates	JOHN W. BRICKER	EARL WARREN
Conventions	CHICAGO	PHILADELPHIA
Birth	OWOSSO, MICH., MARCH 24, 1902	
Death	MARCH 16, 1971	

As the 1944 convention approached, the final defeat of the Axis powers was assured. Thomas E. Dewey defeated Wendell Willkie in the Wisconsin primary, and so Willkie withdrew from the race. It became obvious that Dewey, now Governor of New York, would be the Republican choice. John W. Bricker, Governor of Ohio, became his running mate.

Dewey set the tone of the campaign in his acceptance speech. He argued that the Democratic administration had "grown old in office," and had become "tired and quarrelsome." The New Deal had failed to solve unemployment which "was left to be solved by the war." Dewey pledged, "This election will bring an end to one-man government in America."

Dewey's charges had little impact. Most people felt it would be inappropriate to replace F.D.R. The war was in its closing days, and his political experience could be used to shape the peace to come. Also, F.D.R. was the only leader that could assure a Democratic victory.

The early days of the campaign were left to Dewey who aroused little enthusiasm. Then in September, F.D.R. entered the campaign with a series of speeches attacking Republican shortsightedness and isolationist tendencies. Dewey, in the closing days of the race, became desperate enough to assert: "Mr. Roosevelt, to perpetuate himself in office for sixteen years, has put his party on the auction block — for sale to the highest bidder." By this Dewey meant the Communists, and he charged that "the forces of Communism" were capturing the Democratic party. Charges like this caused F.D.R. to consider this campaign the meanest he had been in, but he was even more upset about a whispering campaign designed to capitalize on his failing health.

Although his popular percentage slipped a bit, F.D.R. defeated Dewey by a substantial margin. In February, F.D.R. met with Stalin and Churchill to lay plans for peace. On his return, however, it was apparent that he was tired and ill. On April 12, 1945, he died at the Little White House in Warm Springs, and Harry S. Truman became President.

Dewey got a second chance at the Presidency in 1948, and was expected to win because Truman was considered so unpopular. However, Truman's vigorous campaign won popular support and the Dewey and Warren ticket was defeated.

There are very few varieties of Dewey and Bricker jugates from 1944, but Dewey and Warren jugates are more common. Considering that Dewey ran twice, few picture buttons were issued. Lithographed name buttons were the most commonly used campaign items.

1—Y—$85.00

2—$32.00

3—L—$18.00

4—$5.00

5—Z—$5.00

6—Z—$5.00

7—$30.00

8—L—$12.00

9—$15.00

10—$15.00

11—Z—$15.00

12—$15.00

13—$2.00

THOMAS E. DEWEY 1944, 1948 CODE: DEW

14—$4.00

15—$3.00

16—$2.00

17—$5.00

18—$4.00

19—Z—$2.00

20—L—$2.00

21—$5.00

22—$4.00

23—Y—$1.00

24—$1.00

25—Y—$2.00

26—$5.00

THOMAS E. DEWEY 1944, 1948 CODE: DEW

27—$3.00 28—Z—$2.00 29—L—$1.00 30—L—$1.00

31—L—$4.00 32—L—$3.00 33—L—$3.00 34—L—$3.00 35—$4.00

36—Z—$3.00 37—$3.00 38—Z—$3.00 39—$4.00 40—L—$3.00

43—L—$1.00 44—L—$1.00 45—$1.00 46—L—$1.00

41—$1.00 42—$2.00

47—$2.00 48—$2.00

VOLUNTEER DEWEY WARREN i'm on the team
49—$3.00

ASSOCIATION OF NEW YORK STATE YOUNG REPUBLICAN CLUBS INC. DEWEY and WARREN
50—$3.00

DON'T BE AN VOTE FOR DEWEY
51—$3.00

Get your grass it's DEWY
52—$20.00

DEWEY WARREN
53-P—$4.00

TRUMAN FOR EX-PRESIDENT
54—$4.00

DEWEY IN 1948
55—$4.00

OUR DEWEY SPECIAL IS DUE
56—$3.00

Win With DEWEY in '48
57—$4.00

MOTHERS · SISTERS · WIVES · SWEETHEARTS DEWEY BRICKER
58-L—$5.00

DEWEY AND BRICKER
59—$2.00

DEWEY AND BRICKER
60—$3.00

THOMAS E. DEWEY 1944, 1948 CODE: DEW

DEWEY WARREN
61—$4.00

DEWEY VOLUNTEER WARREN
62—L—$2.00

DEWEY AND WARREN
63—L—$1.00

TRUMAN WAS SCREWY TO BUILD A PORCH FOR DEWEY
64—LY—$2.00

TOO MANY JACKS FROM MISSOURI
65—$25.00

KEEP THE ASS OFF THE WHITEHOUSE GRASS ITS ALL DEWEY
66—$15.00

I'LL BET MY ON DEWEY
67—$2.00

SAVE WHAT'S LEFT! VOTE REPUBLICAN IN '48
68—$4.00

START PACKING HARRY The DEWEYS ARE COMING
69—$3.00

DRAFT DEWEY FOR PRESIDENT
70—$2.00

DEWEY THE RACKET BUSTER NEW DEAL BUSTER
71—$2.00

DEWEY or DON'T WE
72—$2.00

VOTE DEWEY and BRICKER
73—$2.00

DEWEY AND BRICKER
74—$2.00

DEWEY BRICKER
75—$2.00

DEWEY BRICKER
76—$1.00

DEWEY BRICKER
77—L—$1.00

DEWEY BRICKER
78—L—$1.00

DEWEY BRICKER
79—L—$1.00

DEWEY AND BRICKER
80—L—$1.00

DISTRICT OF COLUMBIA DEWEY WARREN CLUB
81—$4.00

DEWEY WARREN
82—$2.00

DEWEY WARREN
83—L—$2.00

DEWEY WARREN
84—$2.00

DEWEY WARREN
85—$4.00

DEWEY WARREN
86—L—$1.00

DEWEY AND WARREN
87—L—$1.00

DEWEY WARREN
88—L—$1.00

DEWEY AND WARREN
89—L—$1.00

DEWEY WARREN
90—L—$1.00

91–$4.00   92–$2.00   93–$1.00   94–L–$2.00   95–$1.00   96–$2.00

97–$3.00   98–$4.00   99–$4.00   100–$4.00   101–$2.00   102–$2.00

103–L–$1.00   104–L–$1.00   105–$1.00   106–L–$1.00   107–L–$2.00   108–L–$1.00

109–L–$1.00   110–L–$1.00   111–L–$1.00   112–L–$1.00   113–L–$1.00   114–L–$1.00

115–$5.00   116–$2.00   117–P–$2.00   118–P–$2.00

119–$2.00   120–P–$1.00   121–$2.00   I22–K $2.00

123–L–$15.00

124–$3.00

125–$8.00

126–L–$3.00

127–$35.00

128–L–$10.00

129–N–$2.00

130–$4.00

131–$6.00

HARRY S. TRUMAN — DEMOCRAT

Campaign	1948
	WON
Electoral Votes	303
Popular Votes	24,179,345
Running Mate	ALBEN W. BARKLEY
Convention	PHILADELPHIA
Birth	LAMAR, MO., MAY 8, 1884
Death	DEC. 26, 1972

As a Senator from Missouri, Harry Truman first gained national prominence as chairman of a committee to investigate the national defense program and war production. In 1944, he replaced Henry Wallace on the party ticket when Southerners and conservatives became extremely dissatisfied with Wallace's liberalism Less than a year later, Truman became President when F.D.R. died.

Events moved quickly. First Germany and then Japan surrendered. Truman was faced with the problems of conversion to a peace time economy. His popularity plunged, and the 1946 elections gave Republicans control of the House and Senate. This defeat actually aided Truman, for until then he had been doing things as he imagined F.D.R. would. Now Truman could act independently, and he had a number of foreign policy successes. When Henry Wallace left his cabinet he gained the support of many conservative Democrats, but his civil rights stand cost the support of many Southern Democrats. Truman became the nominee in 1948, but many people looked ahead to the first Republican presidential victory since 1928.

Truman was determined not to lose the election and he made campaign trips throughout the country. His main strategy was to present himself as "the plain people's President against the privileged people's Congress." The opposition Truman faced at the Democratic convention was hopelessly divided between the liberals and Southern conservatives. The only person the Democrats could unite around instead of Truman was Dwight D. Eisenhower, and he refused to be nominated. The Southerners left the party to form the States' Rights Party which nominated Strom Thurmond for President, and the liberals formed the Progressive Party with Henry Wallace as their presidential candidate.

Politicians, pollsters and newspapers were certain Truman could not possibly be elected, and they failed to recognize the significance of the large crowds that turned out to meet Truman's train stop appearances. On election day early returns showed Truman in the lead, and to the disbelief of newscasters he maintained the lead all through the night. Truman won twenty-eight states to Dewey's sixteen, and set the pollsters looking for reasons why their predictions had been so inaccurate.

The Democrats did not issue many campaign items in 1948 because the party was split into three factions. Only a few varieties of Truman and Barkley jugates are known. Most items used were simple name buttons.

1—$45.00

2—Y—$30.00

3—$35.00

4—$50.00

5—$50.00

6—$45.00

7—$12.00

8—$2.00

9—$2.00

10—$4.00

11—$12.00

12—$4.00

13—$15.00

14—$3.00

15—$6.00

16—$15.00

17—$4.00

18—$2.00

19—$2.00

20—$2.00

21—$3.00

22-Z—$3.00

23-Z—$3.00

24—$5.00

25–L–$5.00   26–$12.00   27–$6.00   28–$10.00   29–$4.00

30–$25.00   31–$20.00   32–$18.00

33–$2.00   34–$1.00   35–$10.00   36–$8.00

37–Z–$5.00   38–$3.00   39–$5.00   40–L–$5.00   41–L–$4.00   42–LY–$3.00

43–$3.00   44–$5.00   45–$12.00   46–$8.00   47–$8.00

48—$6.00

49—$8.00

50—$8.00

51—$12.00

52-R—$2.00

53—$12.00

54—$25.00

55—$4.00

56—$12.00

57—$8.00

58-L—$5.00

59-L—$5.00

60—$6.00

61—$6.00

62-Z—$5.00

63—$10.00

64—$15.00

65—$6.00

DWIGHT D. EISENHOWER — REPUBLICAN

Campaigns	1952	1956
	WON	WON
Electoral Votes	442	457
Popular Votes	33,936,234	35,590,472
Running Mates	RICHARD M. NIXON	RICHARD M. NIXON
Conventions	CHICAGO	SAN FRANCISCO
Birth	DENISON, TEXAS, OCT. 14, 1890	
Death	MARCH 28, 1969	

In 1948, many Democrats were hopeful Dwight D. Eisenhower would agree to head their ticket. Eisenhower refused this offer, and as 1952 approached he allowed Senator Henry Cabot Lodge to announce that Ike was a Republican. This announcement was all the Republicans needed. Eisenhower immediately replaced Robert Taft as the front runner and was given the nomination on the first ballot. Richard M. Nixon, then a thirty-nine year old Senator from California, became Eisenhower's running mate. Nixon later narrowly avoided being dropped from the ticket when he was accused of financing his career with substantial contributions of money from businessmen. Nixon went on television to defend himself, and an embarassed Eisenhower agreed to keep him on the ticket. During the rest of the campaign Eisenhower remained aloof and rarely spoke about practical issues. The Korean War was in progress and Eisenhower promised "Peace with Honor," but the favorite Republican slogan was simply "I Like Ike."

The Democratic nominee, Adlai E. Stevenson, lost to Eisenhower by large margins in both 1952 and 1956. In 1956, the Republicans said "I Like Ike Even Better" and promised continuing "Peace with Prosperity." There was concern over Eisenhower's health as he suffered a coronary occlusion and an attack of ileitis that required an operation before the 1956 election. His illnesses, however, seemed only to endear him more to the electorate.

The historic Supreme Court decision that racial segregation in public schools was unconstitutional came during Eisenhower's years. It forced him to send federal troops into Little Rock, Arkansas. America's civil rights problems began to come into the open, but the violence that came with the openness was reserved largely for the 1960's. In 1957, the Russians launched Sputnik I, an event that symbolized for many that America had slipped into a defensive position during Eisenhower's administrations. When Eisenhower retired in 1960 he turned the Republican cause over to his Vice-President, Richard Nixon, who narrowly lost the 1960 election to John Kennedy.

Eisenhower's popularity as a war hero and the Republican's enthusiasm over having him as their candidate combined to produce a wide variety of campaign items. Many jugates were issued, but by 1952 and 1956 these were generally designed as large 3½" buttons. "I Like Ike" was the slogan used most frequently on Eisenhower items. With the exception of the rarer jugates, most Eisenhower picture buttons sell for less than five dollars each, and many of the common name buttons sell for less than two dollars.

1—$15.00

2—L—$8.00

3—L—$12.00

4—$8.00

5—L—$5.00

6—$45.00

7—L—$4.00

8—$5.00

9—$5.00

10—$6.00

11—$5.00

12—Y—$2.00

13—$1.00

14—$1.00

15—$2.00

16—$1.00

17—$1.00

18—$5.00

19—$1.00

20—$1.00

21—$3.00

22—$4.00

24—$4.00

23—$3.00

25—$4.00

27—$7.00

26—$3.00

28—$2.00

29—$2.00

30—L—$2.00

31—$2.00

32—$2.00

33—L—$2.00

34—$3.00

35—$4.00

36—Z—$1.00

37—$3.00

GIVE IKE A REPUBLICAN CONGRESS

38—$2.00

39—$2.00

40—$4.00

41—$4.00

42—$2.00

43—$3.00

44—$2.00

45—$1.00

46—$4.00

47—$3.00

48—DN—$3.00

49—DN—$3.00

50—L—$2.00

51—L—$4.00

52—L—$4.00

53—L—$2.00

54—$3.00

55—L—$2.00

56—L—$2.00

57—L—$2.00

58—L—$2.00

59—$3.00   60—$2.00   61—$2.00   62—L—$2.00   63—L—$2.00   64—L—$2.00

65—$2.00   66—$3.00   67—$3.00   68—$2.00   69—L—$2.00

70—L—$3.00   71—L—$2.00   72—$2.00   73—L—$1.00   74—$1.00

75—L—$2.00   76—$2.00   77—$1.00   78—$1.00   79—L—$2.00   80—$2.00

81—L—$4.00

82—$4.00

IKE
NATIONAL CITIZENS
for
EISENHOWER

83—$3.00

WOMANPOWER
for
V
GOP
EISENHOWER

84—$8.00

IF YOU LIKE IKE
VOTE
REPUBLICAN
IN '56

86—L—$4.00

BLOCK CAPTAIN
FOR IKE

85—$4.00

CONFIDENTIALLY
I'M
FOR
IKE

87—$2.00

DON'T BE FOOLED
BY THE
NEW LOOK
ON THE
OLD ASS
VOTE REPUBLICAN

89—$4.00

EISENHOWER
WITH
PEACE
AND
PROSPERITY

88—$2.00

I'LL VOTE
EISENHOWER
WILL YOU?

90—L—$2.00

91—L—$3.00

92—$4.00

93—L—$2.00

94—$2.00

95—$5.00

96—L—$1.00

97—$1.00

98—$2.00

99—$5.00

100—$2.00

101—LY—$3.00

102—$2.00

103—$2.00

104—$1.00

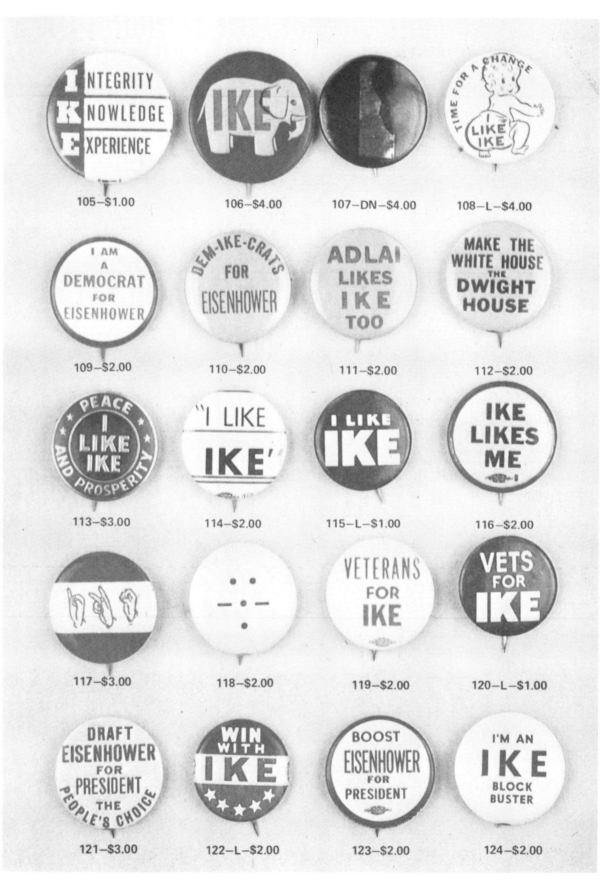

105—$1.00

106—$4.00

107—DN—$4.00

108—L—$4.00

109—$2.00

110—$2.00

111—$2.00

112—$2.00

113—$3.00

114—$2.00

115—L—$1.00

116—$2.00

117—$3.00

118—$2.00

119—$2.00

120—L—$1.00

121—$3.00

122—L—$2.00

123—$2.00

124—$2.00

125—$2.00   126—$2.00   127—L—$1.00   128—L—$1.00   129—L—$1.00   130—L—$1.00

131—$1.00   132—L—$1.00   133—L—$1.00   134—L—$1.00   135—L—$1.00   136—L—$1.00

137—$3.00   138—L—$2.00   139—L—$1.00   140—L—$1.00   141—L—$1.00   142—L—$1.00

143—$3.00   144—$2.00   145—$2.00   146—L—$2.00   147—L—$1.00   148—$3.00

149—L—$1.00   150—L—$1.00   151—$3.00   152—L—$2.00   153—$1.00   154—L—$1.00

155—L—$1.00   156—L—$1.00   157—$2.00   158—L—$2.00   159—$2.00   160—L—$2.00

161—$2.00   162—$2.00   163—$2.00   164—$2.00   165—L—$2.00   166—L—$1.00

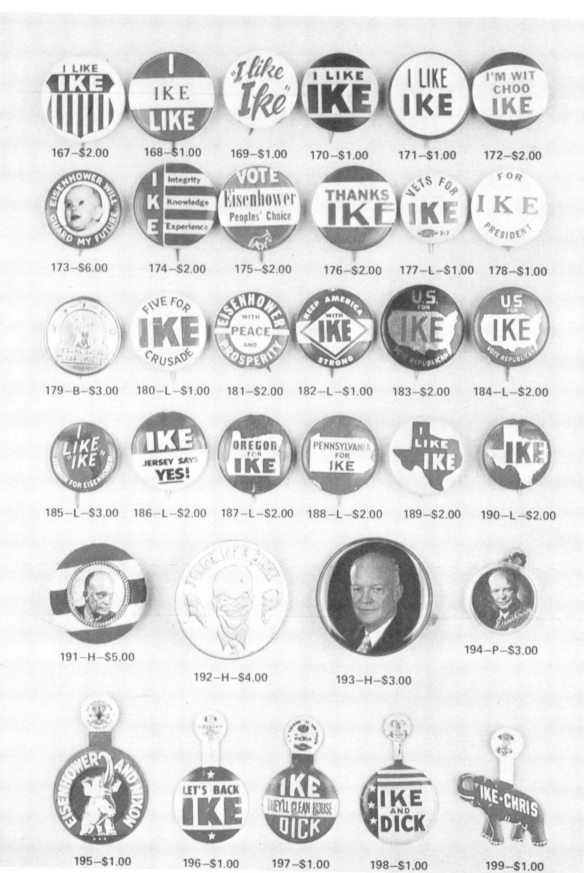

167—$2.00 168—$1.00 169—$1.00 170—$1.00 171—$1.00 172—$2.00

173—$6.00 174—$2.00 175—$2.00 176—$2.00 177—L—$1.00 178—$1.00

179—B—$3.00 180—L—$1.00 181—$2.00 182—L—$1.00 183—$2.00 184—L—$2.00

185—L—$3.00 186—L—$2.00 187—L—$2.00 188—L—$2.00 189—$2.00 190—L—$2.00

191—H—$5.00

192—H—$4.00 193—H—$3.00 194—P—$3.00

195—$1.00 196—$1.00 197—$1.00 198—$1.00 199—$1.00

200—N—$2.00

201—N—$2.00

202—N—$2.00

203—N—$2.00

204—$2.00

205—$3.00

206—$1.00

207—$2.00

208—$2.00

209—$2.00

210—$1.00

211–L–$35.00

212–L–$35.00

213–R–$2.00

214–$4.00

215–L–$3.00

216–$4.00

217–R–$1.00

218–R–$2.00

219–L–$2.00

220–$3.00

221–$3.00

ADLAI E. STEVENSON — DEMOCRAT

Campaigns	1952	1956
	LOST	LOST
Electoral Votes	89	73
Popular Votes	27,314,992	26,022,752
Running Mates	JOHN J. SPARKMAN	ESTES KEFAUVER
Conventions	CHICAGO	CHICAGO
Birth	LOS ANGELES, CAL., FEB. 5, 1900	
Death	JULY 14, 1965	

President Truman announced he would not seek re-election in 1952, and party leaders wanted a candidate the electorate would not identify too closely with the Truman administration. Adlai Stevenson was their choice, although Stevenson preferred to run for re-election as Governor of Illinois. He was reluctant to oppose the immensely popular war hero, Dwight D. Eisenhower, who had decided to become the Republican nominee. Stevenson, a grandson of Grover Cleveland's Vice President, was drafted and Senator John Sparkman became his running mate. As expected, Stevenson lost badly to Eisenhower in 1952, but surprisingly he actively sought the nomination in 1956 at a time when Eisenhower was more popular than ever. Stevenson won the nomination, and with Estes Kefauver as running mate did no better against Eisenhower than in 1952.

Stevenson became known in the press as an "egghead" and "intellectual." He condemned the use of "soft soap, slogans, gimmicks, bandwagons and all the other infernal machines of modern high pressure politics" as "contempt for the people's intelligence, common sense and dignity." While Stevenson's wit and eloquence were not sufficient to overcome Eisenhower's popularity, they did keep him from being belittled as a two-time loser. In 1961, President Kennedy appointed Stevenson ambassador to the United Nations and he continued in this position under President Johnson. By 1965, Stevenson's role in policy making was more circumscribed, and he privately announced his intention to retire. A few days later he suffered a fatal heart attack.

Stevenson and Sparkman jugates were issued in very few varieties, and none are known in the 1¼" or 7/8" size. There are more varieties of Stevenson and Ketauver jugates, but again all known jugates are larger than 1¼". Overall, more Stevenson buttons were issued in 1956 than 1952. One of the unusual 1956 Stevenson items is a shoe with a hole in the sole made as a silver pin. It originated when Stevenson crossed his legs during an interview with reporters and revealed the worn-out shoe. Republicans issued a button showing the worn-out shoe with the slogan "Don't Let This Happen To You."

The more common Stevenson jugates sell for around ten to fifteen dollars, and common picture pins are in the five dollar range. The rarer items are priced very high, considering they are not very old, largely because Stevenson has proved to be a popular candidate with collectors who like to specialize.

1—L—$35.00

2—$50.00

3—L—$10.00

4—$50.00

5—$10.00

6—$55.00

7—LY—$6.00

8—$6.00

9—Z—$10.00

10—L—$15.00

11—$20.00

12—$10.00

13—$3.00

14—$2.00

15—Z—$1.00

16—$4.00

17—$10.00

18—L—$3.00

19—L—$2.00

20—$10.00

21—$5.00

22—$5.00

23—L—$3.00

24—$2.00

25—$6.00

26—Y—$15.00

27—$8.00

28—L—$3.00

29—$12.00

30–Z–$1.00   31–L–$2.00   32–$15.00   33–LZ–$1.00   34–LY–$4.00

35–L–$3.00   36–L–$4.00   37–L–$3.00   38–L–$5.00   39–L–$1.00

40–L–$4.00   41–L–$4.00

42–L–$12.00

43–$8.00

FOR '56

44—$4.00

NIXON IKE I'M FOR ADLAI

45—$4.00

TEEN AGERS FOR TASK STEVENSON-KEFAUVER

46—$4.00

ADLAI ESTES

47—$5.00

FLORIDIANS FOR STEVENSON

48—$6.00

ARIZONA LIKES ADLAI

49—$6.00

50—$5.00

51—$3.00

52—$3.00

53—$6.00

54—$2.00

55—$4.00

56—$8.00

57—L—$5.00

58—L—$3.00

59—$5.00

60—L—$5.00

61—$4.00

62—L—$4.00

63—L—$2.00

64—$2.00

65—$2.00

66—$3.00

67—$4.00

68—$2.00

69—$3.00

70—L—$2.00

71—$2.00

72—$3.00

73—$2.00

74—L—$2.00

75—$3.00

STEVENSON
AND
SPARKMAN
76–L–$1.00

STEVENSON
Students for
KEFAUVER
77–$3.00

STEVENSON
AND
KEFAUVER
78–$1.00

STEVENSON
KEFAUVER
79–LYZ–$1.00

STEVENSON
AND
KEFAUVER
80–L–$1.00

STEVENSON
KEFAUVER
81–L–$1.00

ADLAI
AND
ESTES
82–L–$1.00

ADLAI
AND
ESTES
83–L–$1.00

WALK TO VICTORY
WITH
STEVENSON
84–$8.00

STEVENSON
85–L–$1.00

STEVENSON
86–L–$1.00

STEVENSON
PRESIDENT
87–L–$1.00

LIBERAL PARTY
STEVENSON
ROW C
88–L–$3.00

ADLAI
LIKES
ME
89–L–$1.00

AMERICA
NEEDS
STEVENSON
90–L–$1.00

WE NEED
ADLAI
BADLY
91–L–$1.00

STEVENSON
FOR
PRESIDENT
92–$1.00

ALL THE WAY WITH
ADLAI
93–L–$1.00

AMERICA
NEEDS
STEVENSON
94–L–$1.00

VOTE
STEVENSON
95–$1.00

VOTE
STEVENSON
96–L–$1.00

ALL THE WAY
STEVENSON
WITH ADLAI
97–L–$2.00

LABOR
SUPPORTS
STEVENSON
98–L–$2.00

NO
ME TOO
IN '52
99–L–$1.00

SWITCHED
TO
STEVENSON
100–L–$1.00

VOTE
GLADLY
FOR
ADLAI
101–L–$2.00

FOR
STEVENSON
PRESIDENT
102–$2.00

IT JUST MAKES SENSE
STEVENSON
103–L–$1.00

FOR PRESIDENT
STEVENSON
104–L–$1.00

VOTE
STEVENSON
CIO - PAC
105–L–$1.00

I'M FOR
STEVENSON
106–L–$1.00

STEVENSON
107–$1.00

STEVENSON
108–L–$1.00

STEVENSON
109–L–$1.00

STEVENSON
110–L–$1.00

STEVENSON
111–$1.00

ADLAI
112–$2.00

113–$4.00

114–$6.00

115–P–$8.00

202

116—H—$8.00

117—$2.00

118—PC—$4.00

119—$2.00

120—$2.00

121—$2.00

122—$1.00

123—$2.00

124—$1.00

125—$2.00

126—$2.00

127—$2.00

128—$1.00

129—$1.00

130—$1.00

131—$1.00

132—$1.00

133—$1.00

134—$2.00

135—$1.00

136—$2.00

137—$2.00

138—$1.00

139—$1.00

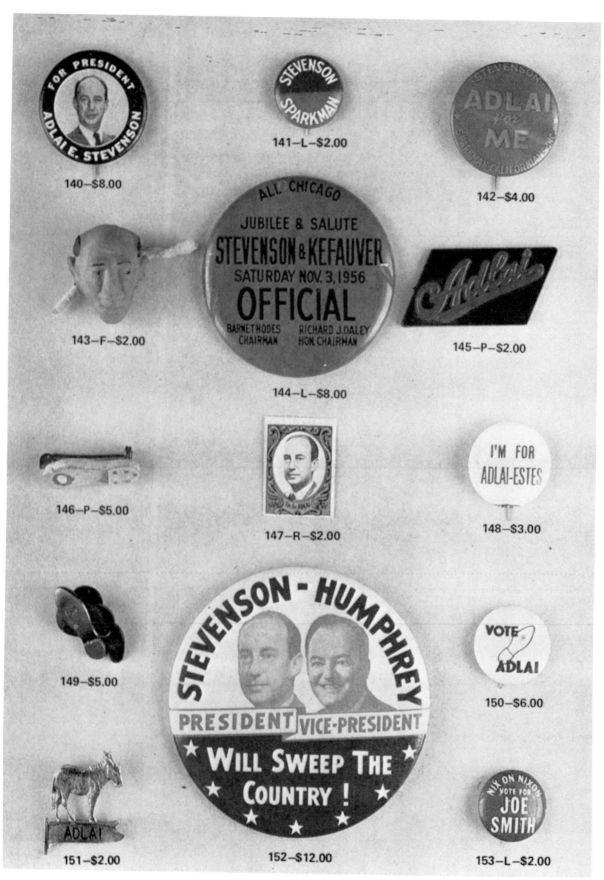

140—$8.00

141—L—$2.00

142—$4.00

143—F—$2.00

144—L—$8.00

145—P—$2.00

146—P—$5.00

147—R—$2.00

148—$3.00

149—$5.00

150—$6.00

151—$2.00

152—$12.00

153—L—$2.00

JOHN F. KENNEDY — DEMOCRAT

Campaign	1960
	WON
Electoral Votes	303
Popular Votes	34,226,731
Running Mate	LYNDON B. JOHNSON
Convention	LOS ANGELES
Birth	BROOKLINE, MASS., MAY 29, 1917
Death	NOV. 22, 1963

John Kennedy had been a Vice-Presidential contender in 1956 when Stevenson left the choice of his running mate up to the convention which chose Senator Estes Kefauver on the third ballot. Kennedy then worked hard for Stevenson and gained the respect of many Democratic politicians. In 1958, Kennedy ran for re-election to the Senate, a position he had taken from Henry Cabot Lodge II in 1952, and won by such an impressive victory that he became the leading contender for the 1960 nomination.

Kennedy's competition for the nomination included Senators Hubert Humphrey, Stuart Symington, and Lyndon Johnson. Adlai Stevenson was also available in case the convention became deadlocked. Kennedy decided he would have to win in the primaries to prove a Roman Catholic could win the Presidency. Hubert Humphrey became the main opposition. Kennedy won New Hampshire, as expected, since he was a New Englander; and his Wisconsin victory was not decisive enough to settle the issue. West Virginia became the real battleground. Kennedy felt that if a Catholic and rich man's son could win in this largely Protestant and relatively poor state, he could win the rest of the country. Kennedy won sixty-one percent of the vote and Humphrey withdrew. By convention time, Kennedy had enough votes to win on the first ballot. His closest rival, Lyndon Johnson, was offered and accepted the Vice-Presidential nomination. This helped unify the party and gave the ticket religious and geographical balance.

The highlight of the campaign was a series of televised debates between Kennedy and Richard Nixon, the Republican nominee. This was the first time a nationwide audience could see both candidates facing each other. Kennedy was relaxed and confident, while Nixon appeared tired and uncertain. The election result gave Kennedy the narrowest popular margin of the twentieth century, although he won by three hundred and three electoral votes to Nixon's two hundred nineteen.

The youthful vitality Kennedy brought to the White House and his tragic assassination less than three years later, had endeared him to much of the public, whatever the practical merits of his shortened term in office. The result is a special interest in Kennedy campaign items which are collected by many people and thus highly valued. A wide variety of items were produced in 1960. Most jugates and many single picture buttons were issued in the 3½" size. The miniature PT boat metal pin, one of the most popular items with Kennedy collectors, has been re-issued in several styles. Many of the rarer Kennedy items sell for higher prices than items from much earlier campaigns, but there are enough common items to build a Kennedy collection from items that sell for under ten dollars.

1—L—$5.00

2—L—$8.00

3—$40.00

4—$5.00

5—$5.00

6—$12.00

7—$3.00

8—$12.00

9—$2.00

10—$1.00

11—$4.00

12—$3.00

13—$2.00

14—$10.00

15—$4.00

16—$2.00

17—$2.00

18—$1.00

19—$3.00

20—$15.00

ELECT
KENNEDY
PRESIDENT
21—$20.00

FOR PRESIDENT
JOHN F
KENNEDY
22—$3.00

America's First Lady
JAQUELINE KENNEDY
23—$5.00

YOUTH
FOR
KENNEDY
24—$14.00

FOR PRESIDENT
JOHN F. KENNEDY
25—Z—$3.00

26—$3.00

27—$4.00

28—Y—$4.00

29—L—$8.00

30—$3.00

31—$3.00

32—$50.00

33—$25.00

34—L—$3.00

35—$2.00

36—$2.00

37—$4.00·

38—L—$8.00

39—$10.00

40—$3.00

41—$8.00

42—Z—$2.00

43—$1.00

44—$2.00

45—L—$2.00

46—LY—$2.00   47—LYZ—$1.00   48—L—$1.00   49—L—$1.00   50—$50.00

51—$10.00   52—$10.00   53—L—$1.00   54—L—$1.00   55—$1.00

56—$3.00   57—$2.00   58—L—$8.00   59—$10.00   60—L—$3.00   61—$8.00

62—$35.00   63—$10.00   64—$4.00

65—$1.00   66—$2.00   67—$5.00

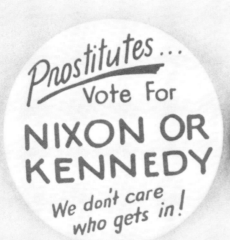

Prostitutes... Vote For **NIXON OR KENNEDY** We don't care who gets in!

68—$14.00

I want **KENNEDY** PRESIDENT

69—$10.00

IF I WERE **21** I WOULD VOTE FOR **KENNEDY**

70—$6.00

KHRUSHCHEV DOES NOT WANT KENNEDY & JOHNSON "I DO"

71—$8.00

CALIFORNIA DEMOCRATIC COUNCIL **CDC FOR JFK** "UNOFFICIAL POLITICAL GROUP"

72—$20.00

I A K

73—$10.00

KENNEDY
ELECTION NIGHT
STAFF

74—$12.00

75—$8.00

76—$5.00

MAMIE
START PACKING
the
KENNEDYS
are
COMING

79—$4.00

77—L—$5.00

78—L—$5.00

WIN WITH
KENNEDY

80—L— 6.00

LET'S
WIN!

81—L—$3.00

KENNEDY
FOR
ME

82—$6.00

REPUBLICANS
FOR
KENNEDY

83—$8.00

FOR
KENNEDY
PRESIDENT

84—$5.00

FOR
KENNEDY
PRESIDENT

85—$8.00

ELECT
KENNEDY
AND
JOHNSON

86—$2.00

ELECT
KENNEDY
AND
JOHNSON

87—L—$1.00

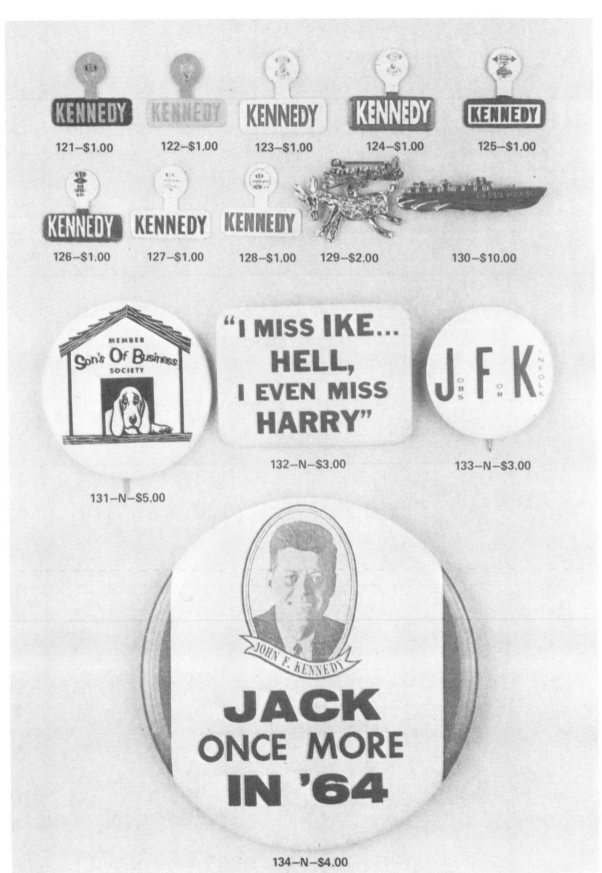

121—$1.00

122—$1.00

123—$1.00

124—$1.00

125—$1.00

126—$1.00

127—$1.00

128—$1.00

129—$2.00

130—$10.00

131—N—$5.00

132—N—$3.00

133—N—$3.00

134—N—$4.00

RICHARD M. NIXON — REPUBLICAN

Campaigns	1960	1968	1972
	LOST	WON	WON
Electoral Votes	219	301	521
Popular Votes	34,108,157	31,770,237	39,295,257
Running Mates	HENRY CABOT LODGE	SPIRO T. AGNEW	SPIRO T. AGNEW
Conventions	CHICAGO	MIAMI	MIAMI
Birth	YORBA LINDA, CAL., JAN 9, 1913		

Richard M. Nixon narrowly missed being removed from the 1952 Republican ticket, overcame a movement to drop him in 1956, lost to John Kennedy in 1960, and failed to win the California gubernatorial race of 1962. Yet, in 1968, following the overwhelming defeat of Goldwater and Miller in 1964, the Republicans turned once again to Nixon. "Nixon's the One", said the Republicans, and with Maryland Governor Spiro T. Agnew as running mate, the Nixon ticket won. The Republicans promised a return to "law and order" and "an end to the war in Southeast Asia." Vice-President Hubert Humphrey ran close in the popular voting, but his association with President Johnson's Vietnam policies hurt his campaign. George C. Wallace, running for President and supported by his own American Independent Party, made a substantial showing with over nine million votes and forty-six electoral votes. His candidacy further reduced Humphrey's strength.

In 1972 Nixon's renomination was assured, and the Republican slogan was "Nixon: Now More Than Ever." Agnew remained as Nixon's running mate. Early in the campaign, men closely associated with Nixon's administration were caught burglerizing the Democratic Party's national headquarters in the Watergate office building in Washington. In spite of this unprecedented disclosure, Nixon won the election by five hundred twenty-one electoral votes to George McGovern's seventeen.

The events symbolized by Watergate did not give the President any real trouble until 1973. This year also saw the resignation of Vice-President Spiro Agnew, who was accused of accepting pay-offs from Maryland contractors and convicted of tax evasion. As the President's top aides faced criminal charges for their part in the Watergate and related scandals, confidence in Nixon himself plunged. By January 1974, polls revealed that more Americans though he should resign from office than those who thought he should continue.

Nixon's three campaigns for President result in a large selection of campaign items. In 1960, a few 7/8" and 1¼" jugates were made, although most were larger. By 1968 and 1972, commercial interests realized the profits that could be made by producing campaign items for collectors, regardless of whether or not the political parties bought the items for official use. This resulted in hundreds of varieties of collector buttons, many of which were poorly designed and printed in dull colors. Many of these items were made in the popular sizes of 7/8" and 1¼" and one design was often used to produce buttons for all the various candidates by simply changing the candidate's pictures. An attempt has been made to picture only those items made and used by the Republican party in 1968 and 1972.

1–L–$3.00

2–Z–$4.00

3–LY–$1.00

4–$15.00

5–$6.00

6–$3.00

7–$5.00

8–$2.00

9–$3.00

10–$2.00

11—$1.00

12—$2.00

13—$2.00

14—$1.00

15—$1.00

16—$1.00

17—$1.00

18—$1.00

19—DN—$2.00

20—$2.00

21—$1.00

22—L—$1.00

23—L—$3.00

24—L—$1.00

25—L—$1.00

26—L—$1.00

27—L—$1.00

28—$1.00

29—$2.00

30—$2.00

31—$2.00

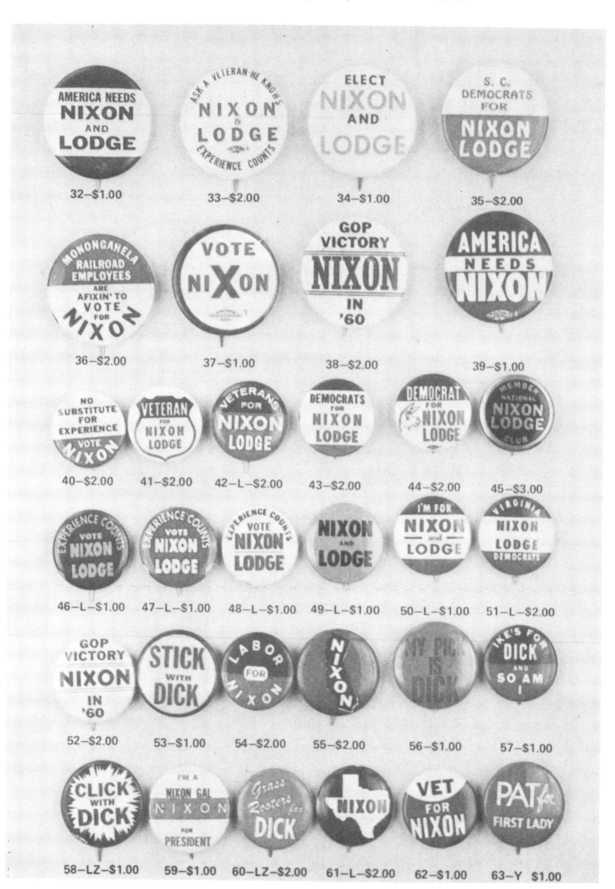

32–$1.00   33–$2.00   34–$1.00   35–$2.00

36–$2.00   37–$1.00   38–$2.00   39–$1.00

40–$2.00   41–$2.00   42–L–$2.00   43–$2.00   44–$2.00   45–$3.00

46–L–$1.00   47–L–$1.00   48–L–$1.00   49–L–$1.00   50–L–$1.00   51–L–$2.00

52–$2.00   53–$1.00   54–$2.00   55–$2.00   56–$1.00   57–$1.00

58–LZ–$1.00   59–$1.00   60–LZ–$2.00   61–L–$2.00   62–$1.00   63–Y $1.00

64—$1.00

65—$1.00

66—L—$1.00

67—$2.00

68—$1.00

69—$1.00

70—$1.00

71—$1.00

72—$.50

73—$.50

74—$.50

75—L—$.50

76—$.50

77—L—$.50

78—K—$.50

79—$.50

80—$.50

81—L—$.50

82—L—$.50

83—L—$.50

84—L—$.25

85—LY—$.25

86—$.50

87—L—$.25

88—L—$.25

89—L—$.25

90—L—$.50

91—L—$.50

92—L—$.25

93—$.50

94—$.50

95—$.50

96—$.50

97—$.50

98—$.50

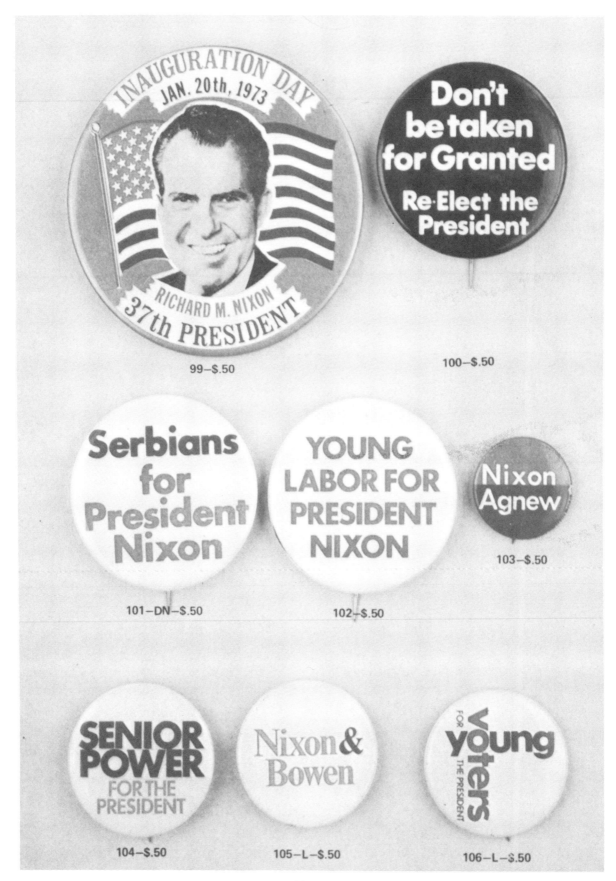

99—$.50

100—$.50

101—DN—$.50

102—$.50

103—$.50

104—$.50

105—L—$.50

106—L—$.50

RICHARD M. NIXON 1960, 1968, 1972 CODE: NIX

Veterans for the President
107—$.50

PRESIDENT NIXON
108—L—$.50

NIXON
109—$.50

Right On, Mr. President!
110—L—$.50

Nixon Now
111—$.50

President Nixon. Now more than ever.
112—$.50

Democrats for Nixon
113—$.50

Re-elect the President.
114—L—$.50

1972 nixon button
115—$.50

President Nixon. Now more than ever.
116—L—$.50

Nixon Now
117—LY—$.25

KiDS FOR THE PRESIDENT
118—$.50

SOCK IT TO 'E' SPIRO
119—$.50

NIXON GOP IN '72
120—P—$.50

LET'S KEEP NIXON 4 More Years GOP
121—P—$.50

Pat for First Lady
122—$.50

NIXON '72
123—$.50

Democrats for Nixon
124—$.25

LYNDON B. JOHNSON — DEMOCRAT

Campaign	**1964**
	WON
Electoral Votes	**486**
Popular Votes	**43,129,484**
Running Mate	**HUBERT H. HUMPHREY**
Convention	**ATLANTIC CITY**
Birth	**STONEWALL, TEXAS, AUG. 27, 1908**
Death	**JAN. 22, 1973**

In 1954 Congress came under Democratic control, and Lyndon B. Johnson moved from Minority Leader to Majority Leader of the Senate. This made Johnson second in national prominence only to President Eisenhower. In 1960 Johnson was a contender for the nomination, but he refused to enter the primaries saying somebody had to "tend the store" in Washington. By convention time, Kennedy had enough delegates to win the nomination on the first ballot. Although Johnson had questioned Kennedy's age and experience in an effort to cut Kennedy's delegate strength, Kennedy went on to offer Johnson the Vice-Presidential nomination. Johnson accepted because both men realized he would give the ticket strength in the Southern states that Kennedy needed to carry if he was to have a chance to defeat Richard Nixon.

The assassination of Kennedy on November 22, 1963 put Johnson in the Presidency, where he quickly made felt his political and administrative skills. His first victory was the passage of the Civil Rights Act of 1964, and this was followed by other legislation crucial to Johnson's proclaimed "war on poverty in America."

In 1964, Johnson was nominated for President and Hubert Humphrey joined the ticket as his running mate. The Vietnam War was the paramount issue of that year. Johnson assured the public that American boys should not do the fighting for Asian boys, and criticized Goldwater's candid opinion that the war should be escalated until victory was achieved. The electorate sided with Johnson overwhelmingly, but in years to follow became thoroughly disenchanted as America became increasingly involved in Vietnam. Johnson's popularity with his fellow politicians and the public was badly damaged. Senator Eugene McCarthy announced he would oppose the President's re-election, and his successes in the primaries prompted Senator Robert Kennedy to join the contest. To everyone's surprise, on March 31, 1968, Johnson announced that he would neither seek nor accept his party's nomination in 1968 and he would spend his remaining time in office working for an end to the Vietnam War.

In 1964, for the first time in years, a number of small jugates were produced. "All the Way with LBJ" was the most frequently used slogan, and Johnson's western hat was pictured on many buttons, tabs, and paper items. Most Johnson items sell for less than two dollars, and few collectors specialize in this campaign.

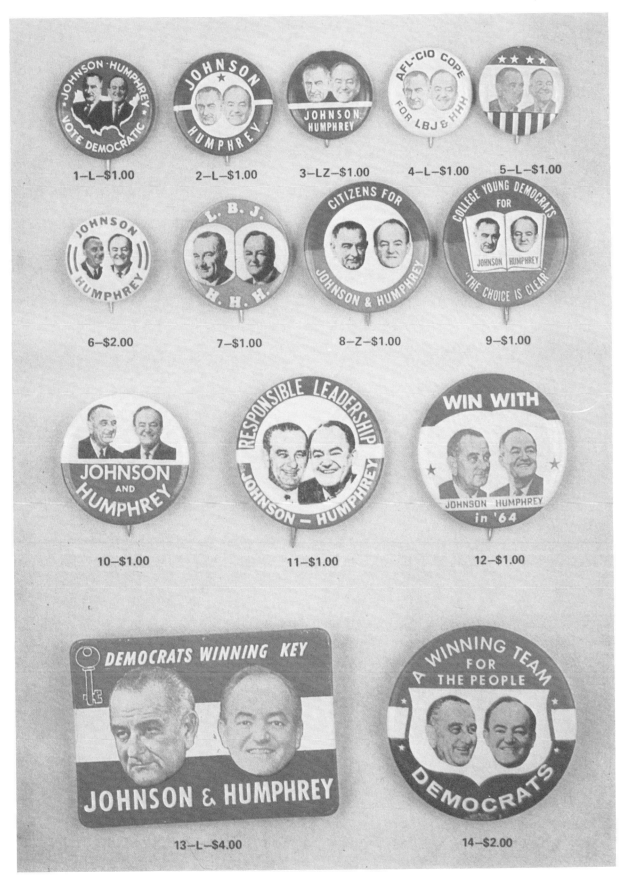

1–L–$1.00   2–L–$1.00   3–LZ–$1.00   4–L–$1.00   5–L–$1.00

6–$2.00   7–$1.00   8–Z–$1.00   9–$1.00

10–$1.00   11–$1.00   12–$1.00

13–L–$4.00   14–$2.00

15—$4.00

16—L—$2.00

17—$4.00

18—$2.00

19—$1.00

20—$2.00

21—$2.00

22—$2.00

23—$1.00

24—$3.00

25—$1.00

26—$1.00

27—$1.00

LYNDON B. JOHNSON 1964 CODE: JOH

28—$1.00

29—$1.00

30—$2.00

31—$1.00

32—$1.00

33—$1.00

34—$1.00

35—$1.00

36—$1.00

37—$1.00

38—$1.00

39—L—$1.00

40—L—$2.00

41—$1.00

42—L—$1.00

43—L—$1.00

44—L—$1.00

45—L—$2.00

46—L—$2.00

47—L—$1.00

48—L—$1.00

49—L—$1.00

50—$4.00

51—$3.00

52—$2.00

53—$4.00

54—$4.00

55—$2.00

LYNDON B. JOHNSON 1964 CODE: JOH

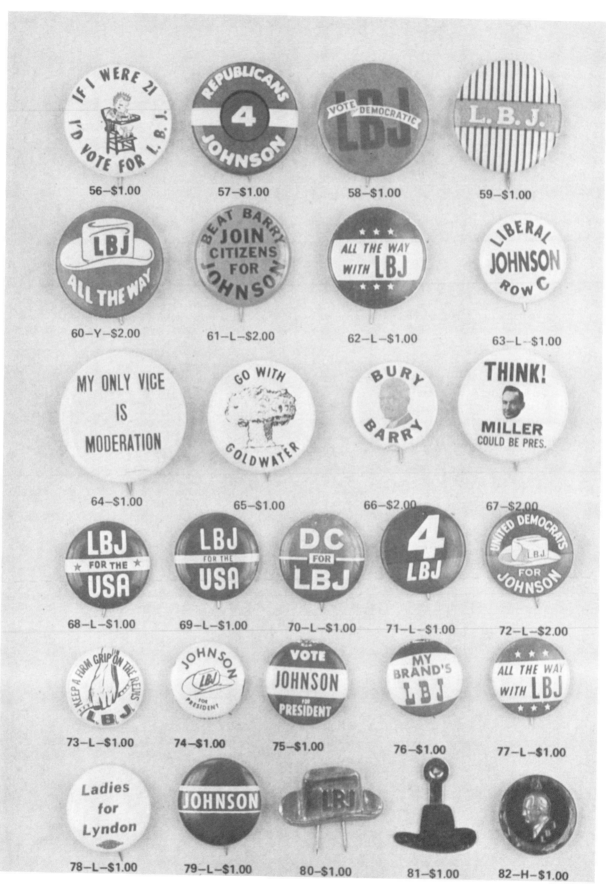

56—$1.00

57—$1.00

58—$1.00

59—$1.00

60—Y—$2.00

61—L—$2.00

62—L—$1.00

63—L—$1.00

64—$1.00

65—$1.00

66—$2.00

67—$2.00

68—L—$1.00

69—L—$1.00

70—L—$1.00

71—L—$1.00

72—L—$2.00

73—L—$1.00

74—$1.00

75—$1.00

76—$1.00

77—L—$1.00

78—L—$1.00

79—L—$1.00

80—$1.00

81—$1.00

82—H—$1.00

BARRY M. GOLDWATER — REPUBLICAN

Campaign	1964
	LOST
Electoral Votes	52
Popular Votes	27,176,188
Running Mate	WILLIAM MILLER
Convention	SAN FRANCISCO
Birth	PHOENIX, ARIZONA, JAN. 1, 1909

Barry Goldwater began his political career in 1949 when he was forty years old with an appointment to the Phoenix, Arizona City Council. Three years later he was elected to the United States Senate, where his conservatism and anti-Communist positions made him the leader of the American right. Goldwater was a Presidential hopeful in 1960, and by 1964 his followers controlled important state delegations. Despite opposition from New York Governor Nelson Rockefeller, who represented "mainstream" Republicans, Goldwater won a crucial victory in the California primary and then defeated Pennsylvania Governor William Scranton's last minute effort to win the nomination. Goldwater selected New York Congressman William Miller, a fellow conservative who lacked national prominence, as his running mate.

Goldwater's object was to offer the voters "a choice, not an echo," and the favorite campaign slogan was "In Your Heart You Know He's Right." However, Goldwater was called an "extremist" and most voters did not share his views that the Vietnam War should be escalated at any cost until victory was achieved. During the campaign it was Lyndon Johnson who appeared to be the "dove" on the war issue, and he constantly reminded voters of Goldwater's alleged readiness to use nuclear weapons if necessary to win the war. Many votes that went to Johnson were in fact simply anti-Goldwater votes. Johnson won the election with sixty-one percent of the popular vote.

The Goldwater proponents issued an incredible number of unusual campaign items. Most capitalized on his name, written as the chemical equation for gold and water — AuH_2O. Other items featured his heavy black rim glasses. There were cans of soda called "Goldwater" and small metal elephants wearing black glasses. A number of small jugates were issued and also a good variety of single picture buttons. Not since the McKinley and Bryan campaign of 1896 was there such an imaginative selection of campaign items produced to appeal to the voters. At the present, the great majority of Goldwater items sell for less than three dollars. The novelty items make this campaign very unusual compared to other recent campaigns, and it is to be expected that these items will increase in price as they become older and collectors come to appreciate them.

1—L—$1.00

2—LY—$1.00

3—LDN—$1.00

4—$2.00

5—$1.00

6—$1.00

7—$1.00

8—$5.00

9—$6.00

10—$5.00

11—$5.00

12—$5.00

13-Z—$1.00

14—$1.00

15—$4.00

16—$2.00

17-L—$1.00

18—$1.00

19—$1.00

20—$2.00

21-L—$1.00

22—$1.00

23-L—$1.00

24-L—$1.00

25—$1.00

26—$1.00

27-Z—$1.00

28-L—$1.00

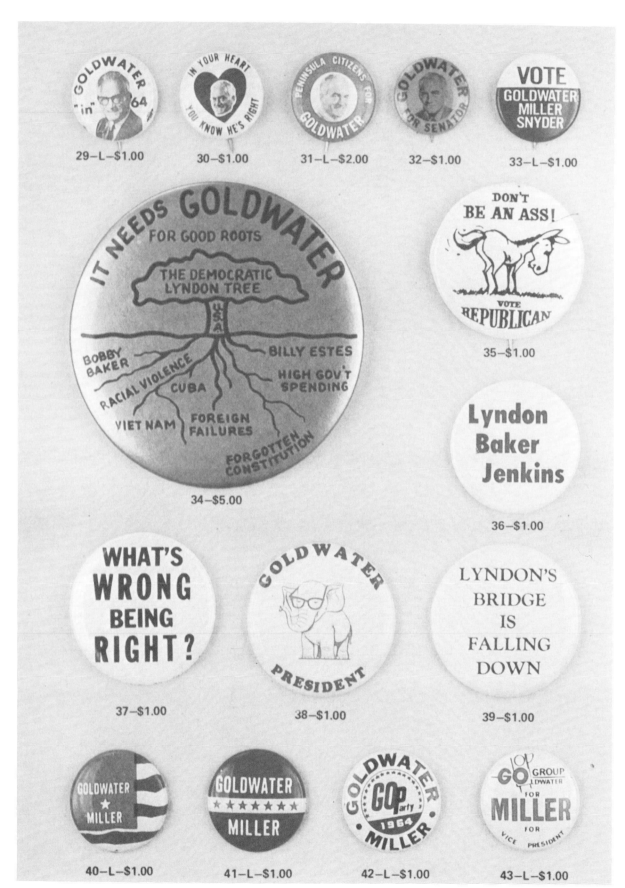

29—L—$1.00

30—$1.00

31—L—$2.00

32—$1.00

33—L—$1.00

34—$5.00

35—$1.00

36—$1.00

37—$1.00

38—$1.00

39—$1.00

40—L—$1.00

41—L—$1.00

42—L—$1.00

43—L—$1.00

44—$1.00   45—L—$1.00   46—L—$1.00   47—L—$1.00

48—$1.00   49—$1.00   50—$2.00   51—$1.00

52—$1.00   53—$1.00   54—$2.00   55—L—$1.00

56—$1.00   57—$1.00   58—$1.00   59—L—$1.00   60—L—$1.00

61—L—$1.00   62—L—$1.00   63—L—$1.00   64—L—$1.00   65—L—$1.00

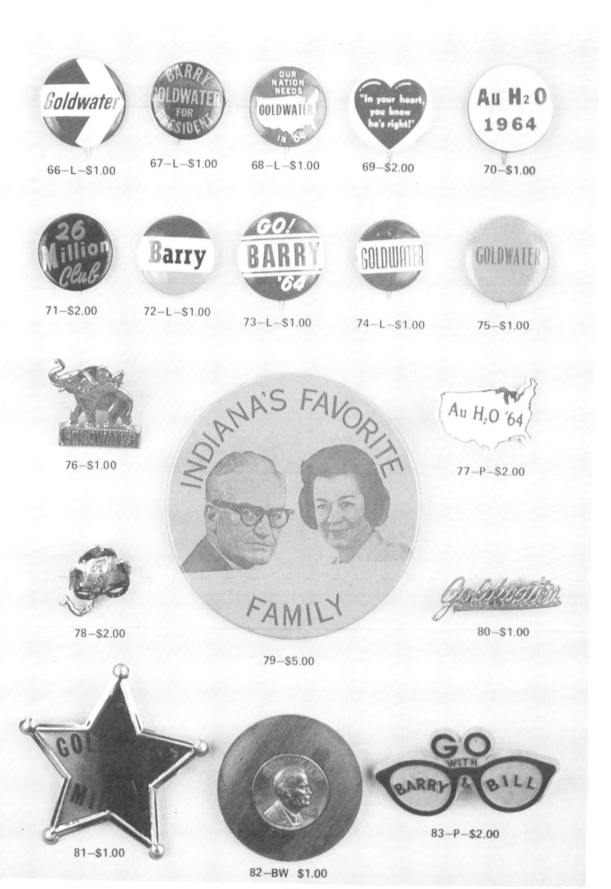

66–L–$1.00

67–L–$1.00

68–L–$1.00

69–$2.00

70–$1.00

71–$2.00

72–L–$1.00

73–L–$1.00

74–L–$1.00

75–$1.00

76–$1.00

77–P–$2.00

78–$2.00

79–$5.00

80–$1.00

81–$1.00

82–BW $1.00

83–P–$2.00

HUBERT H. HUMPHREY — DEMOCRAT

Campaign	**1968**
	LOST
Electoral Votes	**191**
Popular Votes	**31,270,533**
Running Mate	**EDMUND S. MUSKIE**
Convention	**CHICAGO**
Birth	**WALLACE, SOUTH DAKOTA, MAY 27, 1911**

Hubert H. Humphrey began his political career as Mayor of Minnesota in 1945. He was then elected to the United States Senate in 1948, 1954 and 1960. He gained a reputation as a liberal who was willing to compromise in the face of practical realities, and he became a close friend of Lyndon Johnson who selected him as his running mate in 1964. Humphrey was a loyal Vice-President who went on many diplomatic missions and managed legislation for the administration.

As 1968 began, Johnson's popularity was low, and in March he announced he would not run for re-election. Senators Eugene McCarthy and Robert Kennedy battled each other in the primaries, while Humphrey worked for the support of the Democratic party regulars who controlled most of the delegate votes.

In California, Kennedy's campaign turned to tragedy with his assassination as he left his victory celebration. McCarthy's campaign failed to gain enough delegates, and so Humphrey won the nomination on the first ballot. Senator Edmund Muskie of Maine was named his running mate. The usual convention decorum was shattered by the presence of thousands of anti-war demonstrators and the bloody riots that resulted.

Humphrey's main task was to unite the party. Former Kennedy and McCarthy supporters were not the only problem. George Wallace's conservative American Independent Party threatened to take away many traditional Democratic votes. As the campaign progressed, Humphrey began to challenge Richard Nixon more forcefully on the "law and order" issue and exhibited some independence from President Johnson and his Vietnam policies. Although Humphrey's strength was increasing, it did not occur soon enough to save him from a narrow defeat on election day.

The Democratic Party was hardpressed financially in 1968. Very little money was spent on campaign items and those that were used were generally issued late in the campaign. While there are relatively few "official" items, commercial interests designed hundreds of buttons to be sold primarily to collectors rather than the national parties. An attempt has been made to picture only "official" Humphrey items, most of which sell for less than two dollars.

1—Y—$1.00

2—$2.00

3—$1.00

5—$2.00

4—$2.00

6—$1.00

7—$1.00

8—$1.00

9—Z—$2.00

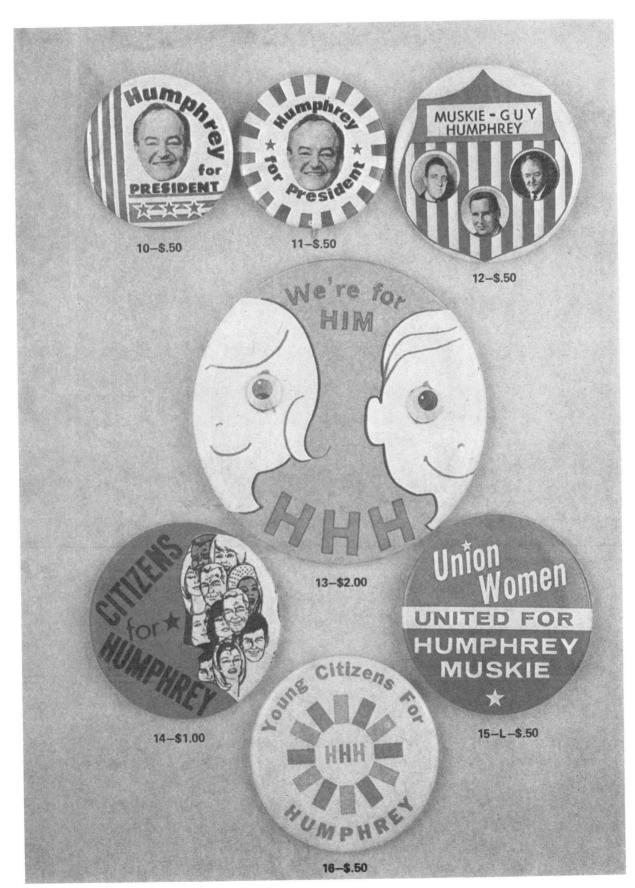

10—$.50

11—$.50

12—$.50

13—$2.00

14—$1.00

15—L—$.50

16—$.50

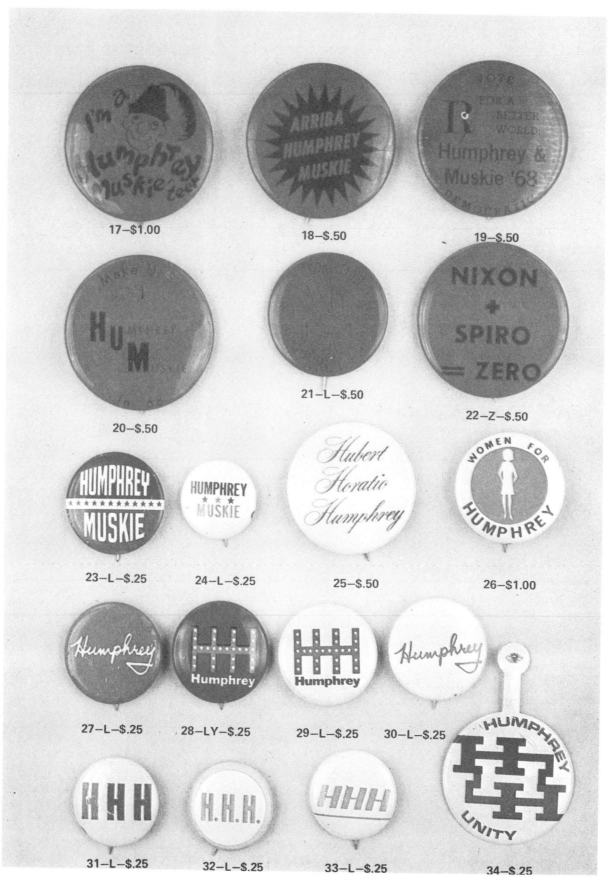

17—$1.00

18—$.50

19—$.50

20—$.50

21—L—$.50

22—Z—$.50

23—L—$.25

24—L—$.25

25—$.50

26—$1.00

27—L—$.25

28—LY—$.25

29—L—$.25

30—L—$.25

31—L—$.25

32—L—$.25

33—L—$.25

34—$.25

GEORGE McGOVERN — DEMOCRAT

Campaign	**1972**
	LOST
Electoral Votes	**17**
Popular Votes	**23,739,708**
Running Mate	**SARGENT SHRIVER**
Convention	**MIAMI**
Birth	**AVON, SOUTH DAKOTA, JULY 19, 1922**

George McGovern entered politics as a delegate to Henry Wallace's Progressive Party convention in 1948. He became disillusioned by the idealogical rigidity of many Wallaceites and never even voted. He then turned to the task of organizing South Dakota's all but defunct Democratic Party.

In 1956, McGovern was elected to the U.S. House of Representatives. He was re-elected in 1958 but defeated in his first try for the Senate in 1960. Two years later he did win a Senate seat and became the first Democratic Senator from South Dakota in twenty-six years.

McGovern opposed continuing U.S. involvement in Vietnam and in 1968 he made an unsuccessful bid for the Democratic presidential nomination. A year later he became chairman of a commission to recommend reforms for the Democratic Party. In January, 1971, McGovern became the first Democrat to officially enter the race for the 1972 nomination.

McGovern demonstrated his strength and the organizational skills of his followers by winning one primary contest after another. The delegates who assembled for the Miami Beach convention were largely new faces drawn from a coalition of interests that included: suburban liberals, former Kennedy and McCarthy followers, students, feminists, peace people and black and Latino activists. The 1972 convention was a revolt against the 1968 Chicago convention. As *Newsweek* magazine reported: "This Democratic convention repudiated Hubert Humphrey, ignored Edmund Muskie, offended George Meany, denied Richard Daley a seat, hung Lyndon Johnson's picture almost out of sight and opened the hall and the party to a generation of irregulars."

McGovern's triumphal nomination was suddenly damaged by the disclosure that his running mate, Senator Thomas F. Eagleton of Missouri, had once been under the care of a psychiatrist for severe depression. After a delay that stalled the campaign, Eagleton resigned and was replaced by Sargent Shriver, a Kennedy family brother-in-law and former head of the Office of Economic Opportunity. McGovern's progressive proposals found little support in the national electorate, and he won only seventeen electoral votes from Massachusetts and the District of Columbia.

Many colorful and well designed McGovern buttons were issued for the primaries he entered and the national election. None of the McGovern and Eagleton jugates promoted as collectors items of the future were issued while Eagleton was still on the ticket. A few official party name buttons and a tab were in use before the question of Eagleton's health arose. There are many enthusiastic collectors of McGovern items. Rare items already sell for more than some of the common items from much older campaigns.

1—L—$.75

2—$1.00

3—L—$.75

5—$.50

4—L—$.50

6—L—$.50

7—L—$.50

8—$1.00

9—L—$.50

10—$.50

13—$1.00

11—$.50

12—L—$.50

16—$1.00

14—L—$.50

15—$.50

17—$.50

GEORGE McGOVERN 1972 CODE : McG

18—$.50

WOONSOCKET'S OWN

19—$.50

20—$.50

VETERANS FOR McGOVERN

21—$.50

come home america
McGOVERN
SHRIVER
1972

22—$.50

"Those who have had a chance for four years and could not produce peace, should not be given another chance."

Richard Nixon
October 9th, 1968

23—$1.00

If you work for a living...
HOW IN HELL CAN YOU VOTE FOR NIXON?

24—$.50

1972

25—$.50

MAKE AMERICA HAPPEN AGAIN...
McGOVERN
2799

26—$1.00

246

THIRD PARTY CANDIDATES

Although Americans have often given support to third party political causes, since 1896 only three of these groups have won electoral votes. The election statistics for each of these three candidates are listed below and are followed by a selection of their campaign items.

Other minor groups such as the Communist, Socialist, and Prohibition parties have run candidates in elections. Their campaigns are traced by showing jugate buttons of the candidates, when possible, or single picture buttons if that is all that is available. Minor parties generally had limited funds and produced few campaign items. These items do make extremely interesting collections because many of the candidates are not widely known and the items are rare.

ROBERT LAFOLLETTE — PROGRESSIVE

Campaign	1924
	LOST
Electoral Votes	13
Popular Votes	4,832,532
Running Mate	BURTON K. WHEELER
Convention	CLEVELAND
Birth	PRIMROSE, WIS., JUNE 14, 1855
Death	JUNE 18, 1925

STROM THURMOND — STATES RIGHTS

Campaign	1948
	LOST
Electoral Votes	39
Popular Votes	1,176,125
Running Mate	FIELDING L. WRIGHT
Convention	BOLTED DEMOCRATIC CONVENTION
Birth	EDGEFIELD, S.C., DEC. 5, 1902

GEORGE C. WALLACE — AMERICAN INDEPENDENT

Campaign	1968
	LOST
Electoral Votes	46
Popular Votes	9,906,141
Running Mate	CURTIS E. LEMAY
Convention	NONE
Birth	CLIO, ALABAMA, AUG. 25, 1919

ROBERT LAFOLLETTE 1924 CODE: LAF
PROGRESSIVE PARTY

1—$100.00   2—$100.00   3—$85.00   4—L—$75.00   5—$50.00

6—B—$3.00   7—$100.00   8—$60.00   9—$45.00   10—$20.00

11—Z—$15.00   12—$15.00   13—$18.00   14—$20.00   15—$7.00   16—LY $5.00

STROM THURMOND 1948 CODE: THU
STATES RIGHTS PARTY

1—$200.00   2—LZ—$8.00   3—L—$10.00

4—$10.00

GEORGE C. WALLACE 1968 CODE: WAL
AMERICAN INDEPENDENT PARTY

1—$1.00   2—Z—$1.00   3—$1.00   4—L—$.25   5—$1.00

1–1900–$90.00   2–1900–$125.00   3–1900–$100.00   4–1904–$125.00   5–1904–$45.00

6–1908–$75.00   7–1908–$100.00   8–1912–$30.00   9–1912–$110.00   10–1912–$75.00

11–1916–$45.00   12–1916–$45.00   13–1916–$50.00   14–1920–$95.00   15–1920–$85.00

16–1920–$125.00   17–L–1928–$5.00   18–L–1932–$5.00   19–L–1936–$5.00   20–1940–$5.00

21–L–$10.00   22–1944–$5.00   23–1948–$4.00   24–1952–$4.00   25–N–1964–$3.00

COMMUNIST PARTY CODE: COM

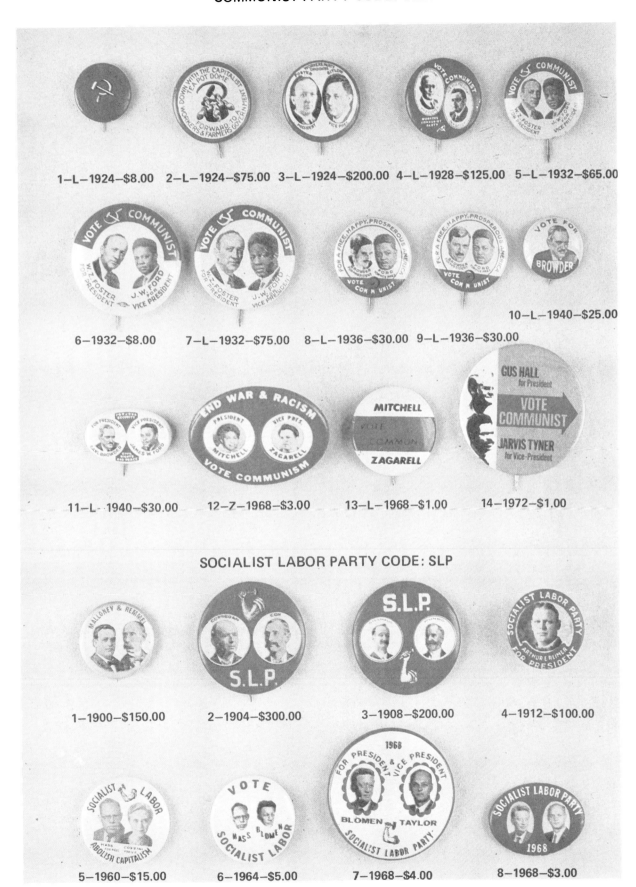

1—L—1924—$8.00   2—L—1924—$75.00   3—L—1924—$200.00   4—L—1928—$125.00   5—L—1932—$65.00

6—1932—$8.00   7—L—1932—$75.00   8—L—1936—$30.00   9—L—1936—$30.00

10—L—1940—$25.00

11—L—1940—$30.00   12—7—1968—$3.00   13—L—1968—$1.00   14—1972—$1.00

SOCIALIST LABOR PARTY CODE: SLP

1—1900—$150.00   2—1904—$300.00   3—1908—$200.00   4—1912—$100.00

5—1960—$15.00   6—1964—$5.00   7—1968—$4.00   8—1968—$3.00

PROGRESSIVE PARTY CODE: PRO

1—L—1948—$30.00

2—Z—1948—$4.00

3—1948—$10.00

4—1948—$15.00

5—L—1952—$12.00

SOCIALIST WORKERS CODE: SWP

1—1960—$7.00

2—1960—$15.00

3—1968—$2.00

4—1968—$2.00

5—1972—$1.00

6—1972—$1.00

PEACE AND FREEDOM PARTY CODE: PFP

PEOPLES PARTY CODE: PP

1—1968—$1.00

2—Z—1968—$1.00

1—1972—$1.00

LABOR PARTIES CODE: LP

1—L—1920—$75.00   2—L—1932—$4.00   3—1936—$3.00   4—L—1940—$3.00   5—L—1944—$3.00

6—L—1948—$4.00   7—1948—$10.00   8—1952—$15.00

UNION PARTY 1936 CODE: UP

1—L—$20.00   2—$10.00   3—$10.00   4—$15.00   5—$10.00

LIBERAL PARTY CODE: LIB

1—L—1944—$4.00   2—1960—$3.00   3—L—1964—$2.00   4—L—1972—$.50

PEOPLE'S AND GREENBACK PARTY CODE: PGP

1—1896—$100.00   2—1900—$250.00   3—1904—$200.00   4—1904—$100.00   5—1908—$75.00

6—1948—$10.00   7—1960—$15.00

GOLD DEMOCRATS 1896 CODE: GDP

1—$50.00   2—$65.00   3—125.00   4—S—$30.00   5—$20.00

INDEPENDENCE LEAGUE 1908 CODE: ILP

1—$100.00   2—$30.00   3—$30.00   4—$20.00   5—$25.00

PROHIBITION PARTY CODE: PRH

1—1896—$100.00   2—1900—$75.00   3—1904—$15.00   4—1904—$30.00   5—1908—$25.00

7—1916—$25.00   9-L—1940—$10.00   11—1952—$12.00

6—1912—$25.00   8—1924—$125.00   10—1948—$12.00

12-Z—1960—$5.00   13—1964—$2.00   14—1968—$2.00   15—1972—$1.00

AMERICA FIRST PARTY CODE: AFP   THEOCRATIC PARTY CODE: THP

1—1952—$12.00   1—1960—$12.00   2—1964—$2.00   3—1968—$2.00

1–1924–$100.00

1–1956–$5.00

2–L–$1956–$4.00

3–1956–$5.00

1–1948–$12.00
CODE: VP

1–L–1960–$2.00
CODE: USP

1–1964–$4.00
CODE: CP

1–1968–$2.00
CODE: CCP

AMERICAN PARTY
CODE: AMP

1–1972–$1.00

2–1972–$1.00

3–1972–$1.00

LIBERTARIAN PARTY
CODE: LBP

CONSERVATIVE PARTY
CODE: CON

VEGETARIAN PARTY CODE: VP
OUTER SPACE PARTY CODE: USP
CONSTITUTION PARTY CODE: CP
CHRISTIAN CONSTITUTION PARTY CODE: CCP

1–1972–$1.00

1–1972–$1.00